Bringing about improvements in the audit market is one of the most important financial challenges of the age. This book examines various possible ways of fostering improvement. It is informative and stimulating. Krish Bhaskar and John Flower, together with Rod Sellers, have a wide range of experience in auditing, management and academia and this shows in their balanced analysis. I recommend the book.

Sir Bryan Carsberg has held numerous senior academic posts in accounting, and policy roles including Director General of Oftel, Director General of Fair Trading and was Secretary General of the International Accounting Standards Committee, 1995–2001

In the 1990s I was asked by the Institute of Chartered Accountants of England and Wales (ICAEW) to help celebrate the 500th anniversary of the publication of Luca Pacioli's 'De Summa'. The Institute was keen to mark this significant anniversary of the key work in the development of accountancy and build the image of the profession in Europe and with the European institutions. My contacts with the ICAEW introduced me to the professional world of the accountant and broke my preconception that this was a domain of stuffy bookkeepers. Here was a world of financial magicians with integrity. Some 25 years later, many traditional viewpoints are under searching examination and Professor Krish Bhaskar's eminently readable, and for the layman very understandable, examination of the audit market is an essential read for all those who are seeking wisdom about what today's accountants are up to and the major issues facing the profession. It is a balanced account, drawing on ranges of opinion from academics, professionals and regulators alike. An important book for today.

Bill Martin, former Head of Single Market information, European Commission, Brussels; Former Commission Representative in Malta; Commissioner General for the EU, EXPO98 Lisbon

Having held senior financial positions in the Middle East for several years, where I have found auditing standards of the Big Four are still of poor quality and very often with auditors' independence undermined by conflicts of interest, Professor Krish Bhaskar's factual research, detailed analyses and conclusions in this eye-opening book, should be a wake-up call to the accountancy profession and the regulatory authorities, not just in the UK, but internationally. This balanced and thought-provoking work deserves urgent attention to protect both investors and the reputation of the accountancy profession.

Vaiz Karamatullah, former CFO of Arab conglomerates in various Middle Eastern countries; presently Trustee of The Graham Layton Trust, a UK charity supporting free eye care overseas

Disruption in the Audit Market

Focussing on the dominance of the Big Four auditing firms – PwC, EY, Deloitte and KPMG – this concise volume provides an authoritative critical assessment of the state and future of the audit market, currently the subject of much debate and the focus of significant government enquiries. Drawing on extensive research and a vast collection of evidence from interviews with insiders, experts and users, it explores the key issues of audit quality, independence, choice and the growing expectation gap.

Just as disruptive technologies are overturning other established sectors, this book explores their impact on accounting, financial reporting and auditing. It questions whether the Big Four-dominated audit market is prepared not only for the inevitable disruption of new technologies, but also the challenges of negative public perceptions, cynicism about regulation and demands for greater transparency.

In the context of increasing high-profile corporate failures, this book provides a compelling scrutiny of the industry's failings and present difficulties, and the impact of future disruption. At this crucial time, it will be of great interest to students, researchers and professionals in accounting and auditing, as well as policy makers and regulators.

Krish Bhaskar was founding Professor of Accounting at the University of East Anglia, UK and previously held positions at the London School of Economics and the University of Bristol. He is the author of over 50 books and has also worked extensively in the IT, consulting, investment banking, automotive and forecasting sectors.

John Flower, now retired, was formerly Professor of Accounting at the University of Bristol and Director of the Centre for Research in European Accounting, Brussels.

Rod Sellers, OBE, FCA, has spent almost 50 years in senior financial and corporate roles in industry.

Disruptions in Financial Reporting and Auditing
Edited by Krish Bhaskar

Following the global financial crisis and the growing number of major corporate collapses and financial scandals, confidence in the corporate sector and, more importantly, the professionals who audit them, is at an all-time low. Based on the authors' extensive experience and unique research (including interviews with hundreds of professionals, regulators and whistle-blowers) this topical series provides a uniquely accessible insight into the criticisms and challenges currently facing the financial reporting and auditing industry, and examines possible solutions.

At a time of unprecedented scrutiny and technological change, the four complementary volumes (*Disruption in the Audit Market: The Future of the Big Four*; *Financial Failures and Corporate Scandals: From Enron to Carillion*; *Disruption in Financial Reporting* and *Disruption in Auditing*) critically examine the key debates, drawing on expert opinions from top industry professionals. Together the four volumes combine into an unparalleled contemporary overview and evaluate the future challenges facing this vital part of our economy and society.

Disruption in the Audit Market
The Future of the Big Four
Krish Bhaskar and John Flower

Financial Failures and Corporate Scandals
From Enron to Carillion
Krish Bhaskar and John Flower

For more information about this series, please visit: www.routledge.com/ Disruptions-in-Financial-Reporting-and-Auditing/book-series/DFRA

Or

See the online companion volume with current updates: http://www.fin-rep.org/

Disruption in the Audit Market

The Future of the Big Four

Krish Bhaskar and John Flower with contributions from Rod Sellers

Routledge
Taylor & Francis Group

LONDON AND NEW YORK

First published 2019
by Routledge
2 Park Square, Milton Park, Abingdon, Oxon OX14 4RN

and by Routledge
52 Vanderbilt Avenue, New York, NY 10017

Routledge is an imprint of the Taylor & Francis Group, an informa business

© 2019 Krish Bhaskar and John Flower

The right of Krish Bhaskar and John Flower to be identified as
authors of this work has been asserted by them in accordance with
sections 77 and 78 of the Copyright, Designs and Patents Act 1988.

British Library Cataloguing-in-Publication Data
A catalogue record for this book is available from the British Library

Library of Congress Cataloging-in-Publication Data
A catalog record for this book has been requested

ISBN: 978-0-367-22066-2 (hbk)
ISBN: 978-0-429-27061-1 (ebk)

Typeset in Bembo
by Apex CoVantage, LLC

Contents

1 About this book

What is this book about?

This book is a concise and accessible guide to the current state of the audit market, exploring not only its failings and how it needs to change to address numerous existing challenges, but also the disruptive challenges of the future.

The Competition and Markets Authority (CMA) and Kingman report were published post-publication. Reactions to the CMA on the audit market and the Kingman report on the replacement of the Financial Reporting Council (FRC) can be found in the online companion volume www.fin-rep.org.

Just as disruptive technologies have played their part in changing the world, through such sites as Amazon, Uber and Airbnb, disruption is starting to appear in accounting, financial reporting, corporate reporting and auditing. This book deals with one branch of auditing disruption. That is the dominance of the Big Four accounting/auditing firms PwC, EY, Deloitte and KPMG who have now branched out into consultancy but still have a stranglehold over the FTSE 350,[1] the UK's largest 350 companies by market capitalization.

The Big Four was previously the Big Five and included Arthur Anderson. All three of us had some connection with Arthur Andersen in the past as did many of our students. Their consulting arm, Andersen Consulting, ultimately became the world's leading consulting firm, Accenture, with fees of close to $40 billion. The scandals that caused the break-up of Arthur Andersen (and there is no doubt that in this case the auditors were to blame) not only led to the collapse of the company, but more importantly provoked increased regulation intended to protect auditors' objectivity. In an environment where competition is limited, auditor objectivity remains a key issue. Moreover, auditors are paid by the firms they are scrutinizing, rather than the investors who in theory they serve. The tighter rules introduced post-Arthur Andersen have had some success: measures of audit quality are improving. But the audit market is under threat more than ever before.

Disruption can develop in a number of ways, none of which, we think, the sector and profession is adequately prepared for. This is not just technology driven, but also the combined effect of a number of factors. For example, changing attitudes in openness and transparency, public perceptions, continued failures or what appears to be a misstatement of financial results despite the continuing actions of regulatory authorities – and the auditors giving what is in effect a clean bill of health.

Definitions

External auditing is an examination and verification of accounts and records, especially of financial accounts, by an appropriate body and is usually determined by legislation of a controlling body. External auditing acts as an important external check and balance. In simple terms, it provides a stamp of approval, usually signalled by a pass or fail audit opinion. In the UK this is mainly overseen by the FRC and to a lesser extent the FCA (Financial Conduct Authority).

In the US, the SEC, and its offshoot the PCAOB (the Public Company Accounting Oversight Board), and the Financial Accounting Standards Board (FASB) provide the same functions. In Europe it is determined by each national government in conjunction with EU directives and regulations. In this book, internal auditing is part of management and the internal controls, so when we refer to auditors, we are referring to external auditors or the process of external auditing.

The current auditing market

In this concise text, we deal solely with the audit market and the future of the Big Four. All three authors come from an auditing background and have consulted widely with the Big Four, the FRC and many others. We recognize that it is often too easy to criticize the auditing profession rather than the origin of the problem, which is the management and the preparers of the report or message. Nevertheless, we believe the Big Four have to change to address the expectations gap, and we recognize that their dominance, and the perception of too little competition has to change. Moreover, the nature of audit must change. The status quo is no longer viable.

However, any criticism of the Big Four needs to be seen in context of thousands of successful audits every year. The British accountancy profession is arguably akin to a national treasure and we should be proud of the sector. Whilst reducing the number of scandals to zero is probably never achievable, we are sure they can be minimized. This will only be achieved if all of those involved in the publication of reports and financial statements – preparers and auditors alike – are faced with a fair and proper disciplinary regime.

So the approach of this book is that it is better to criticize the auditing market and suggest realistic solutions. We strongly believe that the Big Four can adapt and survive in this current disruptive world. But without change they will not avoid the sort of disruptive takeovers that shops, taxis and hotels have faced. It is their choice: evolve or become extinct. The combination of failures in practice and the potential of disruptive technology poses an existential threat. Artificial intelligence (AI) systems mean that the audit functions of the Big Four will only need a fraction of their size, *ceteris paribus*, quite quickly. Standardized auditing AIs will mean that much smaller firms can undertake the auditing work of a FTSE 100, possibly threatening the Big Four's monopoly.

This may sounds dramatic but as members of the accountancy profession, we want the profession to perform a vital, useful and transparent function, and to catch problems like Carillion. In our opinion, it was possible for both internal and external auditors to have warned the public as early as early 2016. That might not have saved the company but it would have allowed more people more time to adjust and it would have been fairer and more honest. Like the medical profession, we believe accountants and auditors should have a duty to the truth that circumvents any client relationship. The auditor's independence is being questioned. If the government is not satisfied, the function of the external auditor could be legislated away to other bodies.

Carillion – a pivotal event

Although there had been previous company failures, the one single most challenging and pivotal occurrence to face the audit market was the failure of Carillion at the beginning of 2018. The failure left a mountain of debt, job losses in the thousands, a giant pension deficit and hundreds of millions of pounds of unfinished public contracts with vast ongoing costs to the UK taxpayer. How could a company that was signed off by KPMG as a going concern in Spring 2017 crash into liquidation with a reported £5+ billion of liabilities and just £29m left in cash a few months later? (See online Appendix 1.01.1.)

The decline in audit quality

Before discussing the FRC verified decline in audit quality, there is the counterargument that the scope, depth and extent of the audit has been increasing year by year. Therefore, it may not be possible to measure quality exactly over time. Yet there is no hiding the fact of the current set of company failures not commented on or found by the auditors.

Stephen Haddrill, ex-chief executive of the FRC, said the UK's CMA (Competition and Markets Authority) should investigate the case for 'audit-only' firms in an effort to bolster competition and stamp out conflicts of interest in the sector. The radical idea would force the Big Four firms – Deloitte, EY, KPMG and PwC – to spin off their UK audit arms into separate businesses. Mr Haddrill's intervention follows a string of corporate accounting scandals, ranging from Carillion to Steinhoff in South Africa and Petrobras in Brazil. "There is a loss of confidence in audit and I think that the industry needs to address that urgently", he said. "In some circles, there is a crisis of confidence."[2]

Audits on Carillion were criticized in the Select Committee early in 2018 as "a colossal waste of time"[3] and suggested the auditors had a role to play in the collapse of the company. The chair of the business energy and industrial strategy said: "We heard from auditors who don't attend audit meetings, fail to visit projects which they themselves say are at risk, and who provide clarity only about what is not included in an audit rather than what is."[4]

Carillion and the other audit failures will be analyzed in detail in a separate volume. However, even this brief overview shows that much is left to be desired from current audit practice, despite attempts to improve quality. It appears the way that the current audit sector is configured makes it unable to cope with current economic and disruptive conditions. This is what the FRC said in June 2018:[5]

> The Big Four audit practices must act swiftly to reverse the decline in this year's audit inspection results if they are to achieve the targets for audit quality set by the Financial Reporting Council (FRC). . . . Across the Big 4, the fall in quality is due to a number of factors, including a failure to challenge management and show appropriate scepticism across their audits, poorer results for audits of banks. There has been an unacceptable deterioration in quality at one firm, KPMG. 50% of KPMG's FTSE 350 audits required more than just limited improvements, compared to 35% in the previous year. As a result, KPMG will be subject to increased scrutiny by the FRC.

Stephen Haddrill, the FRC's ex-CEO said,

> At a time when public trust in business and in audit is in the spotlight, the Big 4 must improve the quality of their audits and do so

quickly. They must address urgently several factors that are vital to audit, including the level of challenge and scepticism by auditors, in particular in their bank audits. We also expect improvements in group audits and in the audit of pension balances. Firms must strenuously renew their efforts to improve audit quality to meet the legitimate expectation of investors and other stakeholders.[6]

The FRC is not without its own critics, but in essence it has noticed a fall in audit quality. We maintain that fall is due to the convergence of a number of factors:

- Continuing austerity policies eroding government expenditure (and those firms depending on public spending);
- Brexit changing the focus for firms, rapid fluctuations in sterling;
- Low interest rates (which traps highly geared firms or causes higher leverage) into a false sense of security;
- The disruptive effect of new technology, internet and IT in general.

Michael Izza, Chief Executive at ICAEW (the Institute of Chartered Accountants in England and Wales, the premier English institute for chartered accountants who dominate the professional audit market) said in June, 2018:[7]

> [This report coupled with the publication of the FRC's enquiries into the audits of Quindell and BHS] has reinforced my view that the profession is at a watershed moment. The trust that investors and others place in us to get things right has been brought into question. We not only need to regain that trust but, in my view, we also have to ask ourselves whether or not the services we provide are still fit for purpose. If we have a situation whereby politicians, regulators and society expect something more from us, and the product and service that we delivered is no longer regarded as sufficient, we need to engage to see whether or not that can be changed.

The joint Select Committee's (Business, Energy and Industrial Strategy and Work and Pensions Committees) report on Carillion[8] was more measured. Two paragraphs are notable:

> 124. KPMG audited Carillion for 19 years, pocketing £29 million in the process. Not once during that time did they qualify their audit opinion on the financial statements, instead signing off the figures put in front of them by the company's directors. Yet, had KPMG been

prepared to challenge management, the warning signs were there in highly questionable assumptions about construction contract revenue and the intangible asset of goodwill accumulated in historic acquisitions. These assumptions were fundamental to the picture of corporate health presented in audited annual accounts. In failing to exercise – and voice – professional scepticism towards Carillion's aggressive accounting judgements, KPMG was complicit in them. It should take its own share of responsibility for the consequences.

146. The FRC was far too passive in relation to Carillion's financial reporting. It should have followed up its identification of several failings in Carillion's 2015 accounts with subsequent monitoring. Its limited intervention in July 2017 clearly failed to deter the company in persisting with its over-optimistic presentation of financial information. The FRC was instead happy to walk away after securing box-ticking disclosures of information. It was timid in challenging Carillion on the inadequate and questionable nature of the financial information it provided and wholly ineffective in taking to task the auditors who had responsibility for ensuring their veracity.

In paragraph 208 of their report, the Select Committee put the range of options succinctly:

208. A range of potential policy options could generate more competition in audit. These include:

1) more regular rotation of auditors and competitive tendering for audit contracts;
2) breaking up the audit arms of the Big Four to create more firms and increase the chances of others being able to enter the market;
3) splitting audit functions from non-audit services, reducing both the likelihood of associated conflicts of interest and the potential for cross-subsidization.

Item 1) has already been undertaken and there is no evidence that more rotation would actually changing anything. The rotation period is in fact more like seven years (discussed later). So we dismiss this suggestion as not offering any significant evidence.

Items 2) and 3) form the major discussion of this book: the criticism levelled against the Big Four that there is not enough choice; too little competition; insufficient independence between the entity being audited and the external auditor; and other issues discussed later.

The team behind this series

Professor Krish Bhaskar[9] is the principal author of this book. He has published more than 50 books and many refereed articles. He has also worked in the IT, consulting, investment banking, automotive and forecasting sectors. He has experience of running companies, preparing reports and auditing[10] – though mainly computer auditing as it used to be called.

Krish has been aided and abetted by Professor John Flower whose major role is as an auditor and researcher into multinational financial reporting. John would probably classify himself as left of centre and leaning towards anti-capitalism and environmentalism. He has published scholarly critiques of the profession including *Global Financial Reporting*, with Dr Gabi Ebbers, Palgrave, 2002 and two more radical books by Routledge: *Accounting and Distributive Justice* (2010) and *The Social Function of Accounts: Reforming Accountancy to Serve Mankind* (2017). He has undertaken substantial research on financial reporting and standard setting. He also introduced modern auditing methods for the Common Agricultural Policy[11] and undertook a number of innovative techniques in auditing what was and is massive-scale mega audits.[12]

Rod Sellers OBE,[13] FCA[14] has spent almost 50 years in senior financial and corporate roles in industry. Rod has given his time, written material and given his views relentlessly, unstintingly and without complaint. But he does not want to be regarded as an author – just a contributor. He is deemed part of the auditing establishment (as he sat on the advisory board of one of the Big Four accounting/auditing/consulting firms) and was financial director and then chief executive of a FTSE 250[15] company. For the last 20 years he has been a portfolio NED/Chairman with a dozen companies – from private family businesses to PIEs (public interest entities). His role has often included serving on audit committees and working closely with the financial departments. He defends the accounting and auditing profession and, although he realizes the impact of disruption, he does not believe that very much has gone wrong or usually requires anything more than evolutionary change. Though in terms of solutions and scenarios to correct problems facing the audit market, he appreciates that something more radical might be appropriate. He also believes that, in most cases, management is basically honest and trustworthy. His motivation to be involved in this series of books is to make sure his viewpoint and that of the profession is taken into account. Rod came to many of the interviews and collected considerable amounts of written evidence (emails, etc.).

See online Appendix 1.01.2 for more information about the authors' backgrounds and experience.

Methodology

During this project, we have performed the classic research criteria.

The literature search: we have examined and incorporated over 10,000 academic and professional pieces and articles on the relevant subject matter. Since we published our first books and articles, there is now a wealth of information online. It is impossible to precisely list all the sources, apart from the most important. However, since the inception of this project in 2012, we have accessed and researched well over 100,000 online pieces and titles.[16]

During the process of researching this book series, we have talked to many people in industry, the City of London, the Big Four Firms, smaller accountancy and auditing practices, analysts, the accounting organizations, bankers, professional investors, including the senior management of investment banks and a wider set of those currently involved. And, of course, the heads and senior management of the groups and companies who are subjected to increasing reporting requirements which are frequently regarded as a necessary evil. We include pieces or views that are attributed to these people. We have also had a few whistle-blowers.

To canvass these views, we have conducted several hundred interviews lasting more than an hour where full notes were taken, many more casual meetings and probably over several thousand emails, short interviews, calls or correspondence with participants, mainly non-academics to ensure that we have canvassed opinion widely. We cannot say that this is a representative sample, in any statistical sample or even in a stratified way; however, it is a cross section of anecdotal evidence from practitioners large and small, professional and other investors, shareholders, analysts, financial journalists, management of medium-sized and large companies/groups and other interested parties.

We have had notable input from a host of academics, partners in the Big Four accounting/auditing firms, boards, senior management, leading professional investors' personnel and less senior personnel from the same. Krish has also been lucky enough to have had a range of input from former students. All the Big Four have contributed in some way. PwC provided much support until 2014/2015. Deloitte's and KPMG have been very helpful. EY have been the least enthusiastic – perhaps wrongly thinking that we were in some way against the Big Four. We are not. The Big Four themselves acknowledge that change is needed – just look at any of their websites. That said, we are taking a longer forecast time horizon in some of our blue-sky thinking (sometimes as far as 2035 or beyond). This is to explore possible scenarios, observations, forecasts, events and solutions: most of the Big Four have much shorter time ranges.

Included as our own text are sections provided by a variety of interviewees including partners from the Big Four, senior auditors, accountants, analysts, investment bankers, other professional investors, shareholders and senior and lower level managers of the FTSE 350. Many have asked for anonymity so there are only a handful of attributions given. Often when we have quoted an interviewee, auditor, accountant or commentator, we do not provide their exact position. Their seniority is not important but, in our view, they are always a person with knowledge or experience. Often they are in a senior position and a number of the anonymous quotes come from partners in the Big Four. Again, to preserve anonymity, the exact wording of the quote may have been slightly altered. We have not always identified quotes separately especially if they came from several sources even though we may have used the actual words from a single source.

Credit must be given to those people who have made much time and effort to provide input to this volume – especially written input. We do indeed thank them very much, though due to requests for anonymity, we are not at liberty to release their names. Many of the ideas here include their input and sometimes their actual words. Where we have incorporated ideas into our own thinking then we adhere to the normal observation to the effect that the views expressed here are our own notwithstanding the comments of others.

Where possible we have also referenced press reports. Usually these articles are published long after the annual report is published but they are sometimes contemporaneous with the failure or event. Most importantly, where possible we always try to provide a balanced view.

Many of the comments we received have been added for balance to reflect all the many comments received from reviewers and practitioners, some of which have been involved in the various cases we consider. Often their response is to disagree with our conclusions in the strongest possible terms. However, our conclusions are based on evidence and are often reinforced by others those references have been given. We add our own analysis, survey data and computer simulation modelling (of which John and Krish have a long history of building).

Other books and volumes in this series

Once gathered, collated and written, this material amounted to several volumes of work. Routledge decided with our consent to split this work into four smaller books. The books appear in the Routledge short-form series *Disruption in Financial Reporting and Auditing* which comprises four volumes:

1) *Disruption in the Audit Market: The Future of the Big Four* (this book);
2) *Financial Failures and Corporate Scandals: From Enron to Carillion*;
3) *Disruption in Financial Reporting*;
4) *Disruption in Auditing*.

Although each volume stands alone, the books are all closely linked. References to other volumes indicate where related information can be found.

Online companion material

There is a comprehensive online companion resource to accompany this series which can be accessed via: www.fin-rep.org. The first item on the site is a comprehensive glossary of terms and acronyms. This (full) glossary lists more than 400 terms. You may find it useful to keep the glossary open while reading this book. At the end of this book, there is a short glossary of about 100 of the most relevant terms.

The reader can access the glossary on the home page and will be provided with options as to where to go for which book with instructions. The site is available as a free-of-charge companion site to this series. The site also contains the Appendices which are referred to in the text. These are indicated in the text as Appendix X.YY.ZZ where X is the volume number; Y is the chapter number and Z is the appendix number. Each book has its own space and updates and new analyses may be provided.

Access to the book's area is restricted to purchasers of that book. Multiple access by several users for one book is not permitted unless licenced. The rule is one book equals one right to access. This is enforced through software. Corporate customers can purchase multiple access licences (see instructions on the site). Use by research students using university library copies may be allowed.

Many of the references are also available online. At www.fin-rep.org the references are given as links to a specific URL. Press Control and left click simultaneously on your mouse or equivalent on the link and you will be taken directly to the reference if it still exists. Note some links and URLs require fees or provide limited access (e.g. *The Times* and the *FT*).

There is also an adjacent site www.fin-rep.com which has additional relevant information, updates and new research results. Feedback from researchers, the regulators, the government, the Big Four, other audit firms, professional investors and the preparers of reports will be posted. Multiple user licences can be arranged.

Notes

1 The top 350 companies listed on the FTSE, the Financial Times Stock Exchange 350 index – that is the top 350 companies by market capitalization. Most of these are classified by as public interest entities which means they have the highest level of reporting and external audit requirements. The FTSE 100 is the top 100 listed companies. The FTSE 250 is the 101st to the 350th top listed company.

2 Marriage, M., 2018, 'Probe urged into break-up of Big Four accountants', *Financial Times*, 16 March 2018. Available at: www.ft.com/content/911e8184-283d-11e8-b27e-cc62a39d57a0 Accessed April 2018.

3 House of Commons, *Business, Energy and Industrial Strategy and Work and Pensions Committees. Carillion.* Second Joint report from the Business, Energy and Industrial Strategy and Work and Pensions Committees of Session 2017–19. HC 769. Published on 16 May 2018 by authority of the House of Commons. Relevant paragraphs or page numbers in the main report are noted in text. Available at: https://publications.parliament.uk/pa/cm201719/cmselect/cmworpen/769/769.pdf Accessed July 2018.

4 Monaghan, A., 2018, 'Regulator urges inquiry into breaking up big four accountancy firms', *The Guardian*, 16 March 2018. Available at: www.theguardian.com/business/2018/mar/16/frc-inquiry-big-four-accountancy-kpmg-deloitte-pwc-ey Accessed April 2018.

5 Financial Reporting Council News, 'Big Four Audit Quality Review results decline', *Financial Reporting Council*, 18 June 2018. Available at: www.frc.org.uk/news/june-2018/big-four-audit-quality-review-results-decline Accessed July 2018.

6 Ibid.

7 Izza, M., 2018, 'We must get this right', *ICAEW Communities*, posted 19 June 2018. Quotes taken from Economia and Michael Izza and reproduced with kind permission of ICAEW. © ICAEW 2018. Available at: https://ion.icaew.com/moorgateplace/b/weblog/posts/we-must-get-this-right Accessed July 2018.

8 House of Commons, *Business, Energy and Industrial Strategy and Work and Pensions Committees. Carillion.* Second Joint report from the Business, Energy and Industrial Strategy and Work and Pensions Committees of Session 2017–19. HC 769. Published on 16 May 2018 by authority of the House of Commons. Relevant paragraphs or page numbers in the main report are noted in text. Available at: https://publications.parliament.uk/pa/cm201719/cmselect/cmworpen/769/769.pdf Accessed July 2018.

9 Brother of philosopher Roy Bhaskar, now deceased and previous leader who changed our understanding of the philosophy of science, through the realist and critical realist theories and movement (*A Realist Theory of Science* amongst others). Bhaskar, R., 2017, *Interdisciplinarity and Wellbeing: A Critical Realist General Theory of Interdisciplinarity*, Routledge Studies in Critical Realism Routledge Critical Realism, Routledge.

10 Although he has no formal accounting qualification he has been an examiner, written books for the ICAEW and CIMA and undertaken and supervised audits

for those with ICAEW and ACCA qualification, and undertaken national and country audits; in addition he has helped one of the Big Four with certain aspects of FTSE 100 audits.

11 From 1981 to 1991. In the early days of the Common Market, agricultural spending absorbed 80% of the budget. It is now a significantly lower share, as the EU has developed other budget lines, but still accounts for 38% of the EU budget of €155 billion in 2016.

12 See above.

13 UK Royal honour: Officer of the Most Excellent Order of the British Empire.

14 Fellow of the ICAEW, rather than just ACA which is a chartered accountant.

15 The Financial Times Stock Exchange 250 Index, also called the FTSE 250 Index, FTSE 250 is a capitalization-weighted index consisting of the 101st to the 350th largest companies listed on the London Stock Exchange. Rod describes it as a share index of mid-sized companies (after the top 100) listed on the London stock exchange by market capitalization.

16 Several hundred with Krish Bhaskar and Rod Sellers present (sometimes accompanied by John Flower). In total, including interviews, phone calls, emails and correspondence we probably obtained more than 5,000 individual views and thoughts. John has conducted his own empirical research with many entities and personnel on continental Europe, and we draw upon studies and original research amounting to several hundreds of thousands of interviews.

2 The accounting and auditing profession

Structure of the accounting/auditing profession

The UK accountancy profession has been a pivotal part of the British financial reporting scene and has been powerful enough to influence the EU and continental reporting. The profession is a vital part of the financial reporting framework and reporting process. Though the power has been transferred to the FRC, the Big Four and the accountancy bodies are an enormously powerful pressure group with a large amount of political and economic clout. They are an integral part of the financial reporting in the UK and now the EU. In the US the only equivalent body that has as much power as a whole would be the American National Rifle Association which has prevented gun controls from being implemented despite frequent non-terrorist massacres. Most of the readers will be familiar with the nature and structure. For those who are not, see Appendix 1.02.1, Structure of the British Accountancy and Auditing Profession.

The role of the FRC

The FRC has disciplinary powers over the top six bodies but not the AIA. The FRC can discipline members of those six bodies if they are involved in the firm or organization producing accounts or financial statements. The FRC's powers to discipline auditors were further enhanced in 2015/2016. The changes make it easier for the FRC to bring about enforcement action for auditors – they now only need to prove breach of a rule rather than behaviour amounting to misconduct. The balance is however uneven in that so far as the FRC is concerned they have to prove misconduct against the board of directors – those with accounting qualifications – in the entity being audited to impose sanctions on individuals in the board/management. One accountant helps to explain this grievance:

> I think the statutory change in the FRC audit enforcement regime for PIEs introduced recently is going to bring about more regulatory criticism. The changes make it easier for the FRC to bring about enforcement action against auditors – they now only need to prove breach of a rule rather than behaviour amounting to misconduct. The balance is however lop-sided in that so far as the FRC is concerned they have to prove misconduct against accountants and directors who are accountants on the board of the company being audited.

So in addition to FRC sanctions against preparers of reports who are qualified accountants, sanctions against directors (who prepare reports in companies) are shown below. This usually takes the form of director disqualification for a period of years.

1) The Directors Disqualification regime to deal with them and BIS [the Department for Business – currently BEIS] does not use it very often but the FRC has signalled that it desires to operate against the preparers of reports. These are rare.
2) More commonly it is Insolvency Service which secures the Directors Disqualification. This was 1,214 in 2016/2017 and 1,231 for 2017/2018.[1] Company insolvencies have been on a generally decreasing trend since 2013 but are now more or less flat. The largest element of the disqualifications obtained by the Insolvency Service relate to non-payment of tax or VAT. Cases referred to the Insolvency Service by the Home Office in respect of immigration enforcement were small but increasing.
3) The FCA can also discipline for market abuse – such as attempts to manipulate the share price.

The register of director disqualifications goes back to the 1940s, and includes tens of thousands of people disqualified from being a director.[2] Some of these disqualifications concern smaller entities which do not have a direct accounting and therefore audit consequence. And many may have nothing to do with financial reporting at all.

Box 2.1 summarizes the various UK watchdogs and their regulatory responsibilities.

Box 2.1 UK regulatory bodies

FRC – Financial Reporting Council. Probably the best known of the watchdogs for annual reports, reporting and auditing. Regulates auditors, accountants and actuaries, not directors (unless they are qualified accountants). Concerned with the listings of companies on the stock exchanges or equivalent, corporate governance and reporting, including monitoring and reviewing the actions of the auditors. To be replaced by a new entity (ARGA)

FCA – Financial Conduct Authority. Regulates listed companies and markets, concerned with the conduct and actions of the board of directors.

PRA – Prudential Regulation Authority. Regulates banks and lenders.

TPR – The Pensions Regulator. Regulates pensions and pension deficits.

Equality and Human Rights Commission. Monitors gender pay gap data.

Department for Business (BEIS). Oversees payments practices, and (rarely) directors' conduct.

Insolvency Service. Currently takes around 1,200 directors to court: may get enhanced powers to pursue directors.

SFO – Serious Fraud Office. Pursues fraud in corporate cases.

Information Commissioner's Office. Covers data protection and privacy issues.[3] Little ability to sanction or fine.

Parliamentary Select Committees. These are not regulators but are becoming more prominent in their watchdog role as an external check on corporate behaviour.

EU changes to auditing

The EU implemented a number of changes which are now part of UK law and despite Brexit are unlikely to be rolled back – in fact they may be further enhanced or tightened. Any new EU regulations and directives are also likely to be adopted by the UK in order to facilitate large companies being able to operate and raise finance in the EU. Whether equivalence, aligned or converged in some way, we are confident that EU regulations are not going to disappear.

EU laws are contained in two devices. Regulations have binding legal force throughout every member state and enter into force on a set date in all the member states. Directives lay down certain results that must be achieved but each member state is free to decide how to transpose directives into national laws (for example time period for auditor rotation). The new European Audit Regulation and Directive (ARD) has resulted in changes to auditor independence requirements.

The Audit Directive and Regulation is part of EU law and came into force in June 2014. The Regulation applied from 16 June 2016, which was also the deadline for implementation of the Directive by member states. The Directive makes amendments to the previous Audit Directive 2006/43/EC, while the Regulation (the first to apply to statutory audit) is directly applicable.

The directive contains a series of requirements governing every statutory audit in the EU. It amends the existing UK law and is updated regularly by the FRC. The regulation contains a series of additional requirements that have received much attention but relate only to the statutory audits of public interest entities (PIEs). These additional requirements include mandatory firm rotation (MFR) and prohibited non-audit services (NAS) – i.e. consultancy services.

It is estimated that there are approximately 350,000 companies in the EU that are currently required to have a statutory audit. Of these, approximately 40,000 are thought to fall within the PIE definition and will need to comply with the additional requirements.

Rotation

Rotation of the firm: all PIEs which are listed companies plus credit institutions (e.g. banks), insurance companies and others.

Rotation of the team:

- Engagement partner cannot serve for more than five years, and then has to have a five-year gap.
- Other senior audit staff cannot serve for a period longer than seven years and then have to have a five-year gap.

Non-audit services (NAS) fee limits for PIE audits

This rule is that group NAS fees may not exceed 70% of the average of group statutory audit fees over the previous three years. As the application does not use retrospective data, this provision therefore does not apply until three years of audit fee data post June 2016 are available.

Non-audit services prohibitions for PIE audits to the entities they audit

This rule is particularly restricting. The regulation includes a new list of prohibited activities for PIE audits: the so-called blacklist of work. In general terms, this covers broadly similar types of activities to those covered in current independence requirements but has a wider scope and fewer exceptions. Of course, there are some grey areas. Preparation of the annual report seems permissible though some areas of that report such as risk assessment may be more of a grey area. But we found that there was appropriate help given to companies in some instances in many grey areas. Examples of what is prohibited in the blacklist are given in Box 2.2.

Box 2.2   The blacklist – prohibited non-audit services for public interest entities

- Management – any service that involves management or decision-making including structuring the organization design and cost control;
- Bookkeeping and preparing accounting records and financial statements and payroll;
- Valuation – all valuation services;
- Shares – all services in relation to promoting, dealing or underwriting shares;
- Legal – all legal services;
- HR – all human resources services;
- Designing and implementing internal control or risk management procedures related to the preparation and/or control of financial information or designing and implementing financial information technology systems;
- Tax – current requirements prohibit various types of tax service: the new ones cover substantially all tax work unless it has no material effect on the financial statements being audited – includes all tax work, customs work and state aid or subsidies;
- Finance – all services linked to the financing, capital structure and allocation, and investment strategy of the audited entity, except providing assurance services in relation to the financial statements, such as the issuing of comfort letters in connection with prospectuses issued by the audited entity;

- Cash – the prohibition on being involved in management activities now specifically includes working capital and cash management and providing financial information;
- Internal controls – the provision of design and implementation of internal control over financial information and systems is now prohibited in the 12 months before appointment as auditors, as well as during the period of appointment;
- Other – there is a virtually complete prohibition on several other activities where there are currently a number of caveats and exceptions, including internal audit and corporate finance.

Auditing firms and their workload

A public interest entity is defined as an entity that is listed on an EU regulated share market. This includes all credit institutions, all insurance undertakings and undertakings that are of significant public reliance because of the nature of their business, their size or number of employees. The Big Four firms dominate: Big Four accountants audited all but nine of the companies listed on the FTSE 350.

There are two mid-tier firms of BDO (Binder Dijker Otte) and GT (Grant Thornton) which are significant. (RSM, though large, comes from a different set of cultural backgrounds and mergers and is slightly different.) This is why the FRC talk about the Big Six meaning the Big Four plus BDO and GT. RSM seems to be excluded in the FRC's discussion – perhaps because of capability or the reasons given above. We refer to all firms smaller than these three mid-tier firms as the third tier. In reality, there are about dozen or so further firms that are small but significant and merger and takeover activity in this area is rife. Below the third tier, there are several thousand smaller firms often with only one or two partners.

(Deloitte is the third largest but in Table 2.1 their geographical area is defined as smaller.)

Big Four business segments

All the Big Four divide up their earnings in a different way. KPMG do not include recoverable expenses from clients. Assurance can include risk management and accountancy work. The only constant is tax (but definitions may vary). For PwC, deals probably mean merger activity plus transactions in selling parts of a company in administration. For KPMG, deal advisory in common parlance means advice given when you buy,

Table 2.1 Top firms by partners, audits and fee income (2017)

Category	Firm	No of Partners	No of PIE firms audited	Fee income: audit £m	Fee income: non-audit work to audit clients £m	Fee income: non-audit clients £m	Total fee income £m	Audit as a % of total income	Non-audit as a % of audit fees (audit clients)	No of employees
Big Four	PwC	953	533	676	351	1,975	3,002	23%	52%	21,864
	KPMG	597	464	548	221	1,403	2,172	25%	40%	13,112
	EY	683	287	442	229	1,677	2,348	19%	52%	13,756
	Deloitte (geo area changed)	719	337	418	214	2,309	2,941	14%	51%	16,732
Mid-Tier	BDO	249	100	151	68	237	456	33%	45%	3,475
	GT	190	69	133	55	312	500	27%	41%	4,629
	RSM	346	20	74	47	198	319	23%	64%	3,500
Third-Tier	Mazars	135	33	47	21	106	174	27%	45%	1,739
	Crowe UK	73	5	29	10	31	70	41%	34%	600+
	Moore Stephens	88	23	24	9	87	120	20%	38%	540+
	Nexia	127	3	15	N/A	58	73	21%	N/A	1,700

Source: FRC plus annual accounts and other data, *Key Facts and Trends in the Accountancy Profession*, Financial Reporting Council, July 2018. p. 39 among others.

sell, partner, fund or fix a business, or more formally, corporate finance, restructuring or transaction (i.e. buy/sell/merge) services. KPMG are the most open and this is further discussed in Chapter 7 when we examine splitting the Big Four.

Audit work, strictly defined as statutory audit work, is probably only between 20% to 25% of total fee income for the Big Four, although audit related work (audit add-ons) can swell this to up to 30% or 33%. But think 25% on average.

Rotation and tendering for PIE audits

ARD also introduced mandatory audit firm rotation so that PIEs have to appoint a new firm of auditors every ten years. The UK has taken up a member state option to extend this maximum period to 20 years provided the audit is subject to a public tendering carried out at least

every ten years. However, because of partner rotation and other consid-
erations, in practice, this is less than ten years – maybe seven years or so
(and five years for Portugal).

An example of the sort of complications this can cause was Unilever
in 2013. Under Anglo–Dutch listing rules Unilever was forced to replace
PwC (audit fee in 2012 was €21m) as its auditor. KPMG won the bid
(audit fee in 2016 €15m). EY did not pitch for the audit work because
it was already a strategic supplier to the business. We consider how the
tendering process works in Chapter 4.

Notes

1 See this government website on the Insolvency Service outcomes. GOV.UK:
  Insolvency Service Enforcement Outcomes: 2017/18, April 2018. Available at: www.
  gov.uk/government/statistics/insolvency-service-enforcement-outcomes-201718
  Accessed July 2018. Financial Reporting Council, 2017, 'Key facts and trends in
  the accountancy profession', Financial Reporting Council, July 2017. Available at:
  www.frc.org.uk/getattachment/77fc8390-d0d1-4bfe-9938-8965ff72b1b2/Key-
  Facts-and-Trends-2017.pdf Accessed March 2018.
2 This can be accessed from this site. GOV.UK: *Register of disqualifications*. Available
  at: https://beta.companieshouse.gov.uk/register-of-disqualifications/A Accessed
  July 2018.
3 Facebook may be fined £500,000 by the privacy regulator after the social network
  giant failed to prevent key user data falling into the hands of a political consultancy
  that helped get President Donald Trump elected. The UK's Information Commissioner's Office is threatening the company with the maximum penalty allowed.
  The tech giant is accused of not properly protecting user data and not sharing how
  people's data was harvested by others. £500,000 to Facebook is something less
  than a pin prick. Now £500m might have been a pin prick. Available at: Bodoni,
  S., 2018, 'Facebook faces U.K. fine over Cambridge Analytica inquiry', *Bloomberg*,
  10 July 2018. Available at: www.bloomberg.com/news/articles/2018-07-10/face-
  book-faces-u-k-privacy-fine-over-cambridge-analytica-probe Accessed July 2018.

3 The Big Four

Size and audit quality

The Big Four: collective behaviour

The structure of the profession is dominated by the Big Four who are tantamount to operating non-consensual collective behaviour. We use this rather clumsy phrase because the word cartel has many negative and criminal associations. There is no explicit collusion over the tendering and pricing process, yet each of the Big Four knows who has won an audit, as well as roughly the price and terms at the end of the tendering process. This is not intentional but it is a small world. There is not any explicit collusion over pricing and terms, and tacit collusion would be too strong.[1] It is simply that each of the Big Four operate similar processes and similar cost structures with only a tiny degree of freedom over pricing and terms. So, there is bound to be (albeit non-intentional) communication.

There is some evidence that pricing goes down on a switch of firm but that once *in situ*, the audit fees rise over and above the previous highest level set by the preceding firm. That is the problem with so little competition. A senior partner from one of the Big Four thinks that rising audit fees are inevitable given the pressure to improve audit quality (as dictated and then judged by the FRC). However, that might be achieved with less competition. As we will see, audit fees are not an important factor in the tendering process.

Often the winner of the tendering process may not even be the cheapest, though we found that any firm being audited can always beat the price down to the lowest tender price. Once chosen there is a bit of a bargaining process. The actual choice is more often made on the choice of marketing behaviour, personality and with whom the management of the firm being audited feel comfortable. See Chapter 4.

However, there is a further consideration. As we have seen in the previous chapter, normally a FTSE 100 company will be using at least one of the Big Four for blacklisted services or other non-audited services (with a large fee that would take them beyond the 70% limit). That firm is then essentially barred from the tendering process. So this leaves a choice of, at best, two out of four possible companies to tender for the audit. If one of these two is also undertaking consultancy work, then the choice of an auditor comes down to one – if no changes to workload of the Big Four occurs. In such situation, there is a degree of unhealthy inbreeding or non-consensual collusion. We will argue later that this situation could be made much worse by technological developments.

The pyramid structure

Big Four firms have adopted a multi-level hierarchy. They give different names to the levels: associate/trainee (junior), senior associate, manager, director, associate partner (sometimes) and partner. This structure is a pyramid with large numbers at the bottom of the pyramid earning a pittance at the beginning of their careers. In fact, the only well-paid staff are the partners. Table 3.1 shows our reconstruction of a typical largish firm – somewhere in between PwC and Deloitte. Although it's not based on actual data it is very similar to a couple of the real firms.[2]

Gow and Kells[3] explain this as:

> Leverage [not the usual financial term which is the extent of borrowing for a firm] involves sending out less experienced staff to do the work that has been sold by directors and partners. Clients complain that those sellers – so engaging and compelling in the pitch meeting – usually vanish soon after the sale is complete, never to be seen again [not quite true as in our experience the audit engagement partner is always around]. The success of the Big Four may have been built on the backs of juniors, but institutionalised reliance on inexperienced staff can lead the Big Four into danger. In the TBW-Colonial case [discussed in endnote 3 in Chapter 9], for example, it was claimed that a PwC intern was in charge of checking billions of dollars' worth of collateral, and that the intern's supervisor was another junior, who thought his duties were 'above his pay grade'.

That said, as Gow and Kells point out, the juniors are the heroes of accounting scandals as often as they are the villains. Waste Management was a 1998 US scandal, significant because the junior audit staff discovered all the problems and reported them to the partners. This case is discussed in the *Financial Failures and Corporate Scandals: From Enron to Carillion* volume.

Table 3.1 Breakdown of typical Big Four with staffing by level, gender and salary level

	Partner	Associate partner	Director	Senior manager	Manager	Senior associate	Associate/ Trainee	Client account support	Support	Total
Gender										
Men	403	360	670	1,100	1,768	2,080	3,640	213	165	10,398
Women	98	140	330	900	1,733	1,920	3,360	288	835	9,603
Total	500	500	1,000	2,000	3,500	4,000	7,000	500	1,000	20,000
Men	80.5%	72.0%	67.0%	55.0%	50.5%	52.0%	52.0%	42.5%	16.5%	52.0%
Women	19.5%	28.0%	33.0%	45.0%	49.5%	48.0%	48.0%	57.5%	83.5%	48.0%
Ethnicity										
BAME	91%	90%	85%	80%	73%	66%	64%	95%	49%	70.0%
White	9%	10%	15%	20%	27%	34%	36%	5%	51%	30.0%
White	455	450	850	1,600	2,555	2,640	4,480	475	490	13,995
BAME	45	50	150	400	945	1,360	2,520	25	510	6,005
Total	500	500	1,000	2,000	3,500	4,000	7,000	500	1,000	20,000
Median salary										
Men	£734,026	£604,213	£125,307	£89,068	£67,849	£45,419	£29,856	£85,456	£26,749	£1,040,536
Women	£556,057	£475,829	£132,416	£83,529	£66,529	£44,859	£27,859	£86,749	£24,124	£579,786
Total	£1,290,083	£1,080,042	£257,723	£172,597	£134,378	£90,278	£57,715	£172,205	£50,873	£1,620,322

Source: Authors

Leverage (in the Gow and Kells sense of having lots of worker-bee juniors) drove growth among the Big Four. They also claim that 'branding' was a further driver of Big Four growth.

> As the four businesses became better known, clients gravitated towards them, creating a reinforcing current. Size conferred market power on the firms, and offered real or perceived benefits from diversification. Professional rules further encouraged the rush for bigness. In the 1970s, for example, the ICAEW directed that no audit practice could accept a client that represented more than 15% of its revenue. In light of this and other strictures, most second-tier firms merged into what were then the Big Eight: Arthur Andersen, Arthur Young McClelland Moores & Co., Coopers & Lybrand, Deloitte Haskins & Sells, Ernst & Whinney, Peat Marwick Mitchell, Price Waterhouse and Touche Ross Bailey & Smart. When the major firms were ranked according to revenue, after the Big Eight there was daylight.[4]

In 1989, Arthur Young and Ernst & Whinney became Ernst & Young, and Deloitte Haskins & Sells merged with Touche Ross in the USA to form Deloitte & Touche.[5] In 1998, Price Waterhouse merged with Coopers & Lybrand to form PricewaterhouseCoopers. KMG and Peat Marwick became KPMG in 1999 in the UK (earlier in the US). Arthur Andersen collapsed in 2002 after several failures, and during this time, Accenture was born out of Andersen Consulting. Subsequently, Deloitte and Touche became just Deloitte and Ernst & Whinney became known as EY.

Trainee auditors as cannon fodder = long often unpaid hours

There is one problem not yet raised or touched upon. An auditing firm will set a certain number of chargeable hours to complete a job undertaken by a trainer. Frequently that number is an understatement of the actual time required to complete that job. The trainee is expected to work the extra hours to complete it without payment or those additional hours being entered on to his or her timesheets. Consider this letter – we are paraphrasing here:

> deficiencies in auditing are likely to occur when auditors are expected to work for 16 hours a day for weeks on end with scant breaks for weekends and holidays. This especially applies to young auditors, with the Big Four apparently considering this a tradition to break them in, . . . [who] had to work on a stressful audit from 9am to

1am for weeks. This makes it difficult to keep up the high standards of work that it is these companies' duty to maintain.[6]

One cannot help wondering about the health and welfare of this pyramid structure. All firms have a pyramid structure but the Big Four are particularly flat with the really large increases in salary coming only when one makes partner. And then there is a hierarchy of partners. But the trainees, juniors and just qualified are not at all well paid by City standards. And now the large tech companies, unicorns and start-ups seem to be attracting the best talent. So the Big Four will be under pressure – like never before.

Degree of concentration

Table 3.2 illustrates the percentage of the number of audits of UK listed companies undertaken by the Big Four firms, the next five firms (based on the number of listed audit clients) and other audit firms in 2016.

Since 2016, concentration by the Big Four has further increased. The Big Four had a 95% share of the audits of FTSE 350 in 2012/2013. By 2018 this had increased to 98%. We forecast this will increase to close to 100% by 2025 or shortly after – that is if nothing changes. As Reuters put it:

> Policymakers have tried for years to weaken the Big Four's dominance. But reform requiring companies to consider switching accountants every 10 years – designed to keep auditors from becoming too cozy with clients – has merely made for a faster four-seat merry-go-round.[7]

However, things may very well change. *Ceteris* is never *paribus* in the real world. The Big Four wants the FRC to be tougher, and others want the

Table 3.2 Concentration in 2016 – percentage of category

	FTSE 100	FTSE 250	Other UK main market	All main market
Big Four	98.0%	96.4%	74.8%	81.0%
Next five	1.0%	3.8%	18.0%	13.3%
Other firms	0.0%	0.0%	6.8%	5.7%

Source: FRC

break-up not only of the FRC, but The Pensions Regulator and possibly the FCA. The FRC wants the break-up of the Big Four, and also wants to be involved in the recruitment of candidates for senior positions at the six largest accountancy firms. And so the dispute goes on . . . Currently, Kingman wants the FRC replaced. The Government has announced the replacement as ARGA with stronger powers.

Mid-tier firms withdrawing from audit

After the Big Four the next two mid-tier firms are BDO and GT. GT withdrew from the tendering for the larger audits in March 2018.

GT gave up trying to win new FTSE 350 audit customers after losing out in the tendering process for the audit of Marks & Spencer and others, where one of the Big Four won. It was "frustrating" that so many audit committee members saw choosing one of the Big Four as the low-risk option.[8] Because of their size and reach, and their reputation, the Big Four are preferred by management. Hence, we suspect that BDO will eventually go the same way. Apart from the cost of the tendering process, there is the morale of the staff to consider when you continually lose the tendering process. However, GT will continue to audit the five FTSE 350 firms they currently audit.

The mid-tier firms have a major foothold in the public sector and AIM market – though the Big Four are making inroads there as well. GT has a top position in the M&A market. BDO says it works for the one-third of the FTSE 350 in an advisory capacity. Both companies have a line in forensic services. The fact that they are not one of the Big Four, in a way, is their strength. Employing one of them does not limit their choice of which auditor to choose, whilst employing one of the Big Four limits their choice because of the blacklist service (e.g. tax) or the non-audit fee limit.

The FT suggests that Big Four dominance will add pressure on authorities to intervene:

> The UK accountancy firm Grant Thornton has decided to stop bidding for audit contracts from Britain's largest listed companies after concluding it is too difficult to compete with the Big Four firms that dominate the market. The decision will deal a big blow to efforts by Deloitte, EY, KPMG and PwC to convince politicians and regulators not to intervene in the market. It will also increase pressure on UK authorities to tackle their dominance: the Big Four's share of FTSE 350 auditing has increased from 95 per cent to 98 per cent over the past five years. This is despite a series of EU and UK reforms introduced since the financial crisis.[9]

Even when the mid-tier firms do win the tender process, normally because all of the Big Four are ruled out due to conflict of interest, then there is a backlash against the mid-tier audit firm.

Acceptability of the mid-tier?

As discussed in later chapters, the US global investment bank, Goldman Sachs, wanted to appoint GT (the fifth largest audit firm and the largest of the mid-tier firms). The Bank of England queried the appointment of GT as Goldman Sachs auditor (from 2022) and the PRA, set up after the GFC to protect the stability of UK's banks, has flagged concerns about the potential appointment, according to press reports. Note that US and European banks were affected as the rules applied to all PIEs in Europe – the US banks lie within the PIE definition. They have to appoint a new audit firm to oversee the entire global business (Goldman uses PwC globally) or select a second firm to audit their European business (and Goldman chose GT because all the other Big Four were involved or had a conflict of interest). That choice is now being questioned.

Niche market means rapid growth for the mid-tier

That said, because of conflicts of interest and the lack of sufficient numbers of the Big Four to go around, the mid-tier firms have a niche market all to themselves. Goldman Sachs can still claim a Big Four as their global auditors – the fact that GT audits the European branches or even just the UK, is lost in the small print. So we envisage double digit growth of the mid-tier and some of the larger in the top 20 audit firms until at least 2028 to 2030 when the rotation and other regulations required for PIE rules have worked their way through all the overseas PIEs operating in the UK.

The mid-tier firms of the future are assured and may grow. New entrants to the current three (GT, BDO and RSM) may be added over time. Globally, Crowe Horwath, Baker Tilly and Nexia look strong. In the UK you could add these smaller mid-tier firms: Smith & Williamson; Crowe Clark Whitehill; PFK; MHA (now split into two); Begbies Traynor; Wilkins Kennedy; Menzies; and others. These smaller mid-tier firms keep merging so it is difficult to keep track of them. In fact merger and acquisition activity is at a very high level. By 2020 or 2021 the Big 25 might have become something more like the Big Eight or Nine (in this scenario).

Big Four future fee income streams and the future audit fee income environment

In the series volume *Disruption in Auditing*, the future fee income streams of the Big Four are broken down and spelt out numerically. The analysis in Box 3.1 assumes that nothing changes apart from a tightening of auditing standards and a slight expansion of the scope of audit work. This does not include detailed forecasting work for enhanced going-concern or viability analysis.

Box 3.1   Big Four future fee income streams

Audit and directly related services: probably increased by 25% to 35% in real terms to cover the existing regulation and a slight tightening of the same.

Non-audit work for the audited entities: probably will not increase other than in line with audit fee income.

Non-audit work for non-audited entities: this has been growing and now represents over 70% of the Big Four fee income and will continue to grow.

New types of audit, reassurance and reporting work: we assume that there will be

1) additional scope, coverage, depth of audit, as well as additional procedures and reports;
2) additional help with multiple reports, and multiple delivery systems;
3) huge expansion with varying levels of reassurance of non-financial information.

We see audit and other fee income rising to at least £5 billion by 2030 and growing to a much larger sum by the 2040 to 2050. This may be shared with new entrants of course, if the Big Four do not survive in their current from.

Consultancy fees by the Big Four

Meanwhile the Big Four firms are increasing their consulting arms, which accounted for 40% of all revenues earned in the UK's consulting market in 2017.[10] They win the majority of the work in the financial services market. Their combined consultancy divisions earned £3 billion out of a total market of around £7.8 billion – though other sources put the total markets closer to £11 billion.[11] Either way we see this consultancy market growing, and the Big Four's share growing to over 50% of the total.

The Bank of England queried the appointment of GT as Goldman Sachs's auditor (from 2022) and the PRA, set up after the GFC to protect the stability of UK's banks, has flagged concerns about the potential appointment, according to press reports.

Size and quality

Does size make for good quality? Are the Big Four undertaking higher quality audits? Can smaller firms undertake high-quality audits? Perceptions and global reach probably account for much of the answers to these questions. This is the perceived analysis.

What is a high-quality audit?

Google 'high quality audits' and you will find the subject matter of the audit of quality control systems. A smallish New England practice said this about audit quality and we agree with them:

> There are no universally agreed upon definitions of high or low quality in audits, no settled measures or benchmarks, and no agreement about the drivers of such quality. It is difficult for prospective clients and other stakeholders outside a company to 'look under the hood' and judge audit quality for themselves, because an audit's elements are often complex and hard to measure. Much of an audit relies on the process of the audit, and the process can be all but invisible to the client and even more so to financial statement users. Indeed, the only outwardly visible signs of a potentially poor-quality audit are financial statement restatements or re-issuances and investigations. But these can take years to surface and might, by then, bear little relation to the audit's original quality issues.[12]

Deloitte's definition in Box 3.2 is as good as any definition gets. All the Big Four have quality audits. In theory the quality of audit is consistent across all audit firms, as audits are performed according to accepted audit standards.

Box 3.2   What is a high-quality audit?[13]
(Deloitte – selected passages)

Quality means a total commitment to making sound judgments. It means ensuring that all the right steps are taken consistently in the course of the Audit. It means providing a bedrock of confidence in the results verified. That is why quality performed audit helps clients to increase the reliability of the reported financial statements and consequently on the possibility of obtaining loans from the most prestigious lending institutions and attracting potential partners for joint investments.

The exact nature of high–quality audit varies essentially over time, into an evolving activity with the development of the daily business environment, financial reporting standards, auditing standards, regulations and technology. This means that the pursuit of the quality of the audit is a never-ending quest and is not a fixed objective with a final result.

The FRC accepts that there is no single agreed definition of audit quality that can be used as a standard against which actual performance can be measured. Instead they believe that the following are key drivers of quality:

- The culture within an audit firm;
- The skills and personal qualities of audit partners and staff;
- The effectiveness of the audit process;
- The reliability and usefulness of audit reporting;
- Factors outside the control of auditors affecting audit quality.

DeAngelo[14]

She was first to argue that quality and size were correlated:

the current paper argues that audit quality is not independent of audit firm size, even when auditors initially possesses identical technological capabilities. In particular, when incumbent auditors earn client-specific quasi-rents, auditors with a greater number of clients have 'more to lose' by failing to report a discovered breach in a particular client's records. This collateral aspect increases the audit quality supplied by larger audit firms. The implications for some recent recommendations of the AICPA Special Committee on Small and Medium Sized Firms are developed.

ACCA study[15]

The study assessed the perceptions of directors, financial directors/CFOs and auditors against the relative importance of a number of attributes.

Of the three groups in the study, auditors have the most information available to them about audit quality, directors the least, and CFOs are somewhere in between.

Even so, the report's authors were surprised to find a high level of agreement between the three stakeholder groups on what contributes to a high quality audit.

In fact, all three groups ranked the competence of the firm and its team and the interaction between the company and auditor as more important than independence. Auditors, CFOs and directors ranked audit firm size as the most important attribute as an indicator of audit quality, followed by the level of attention that partners and managers paid to the audit. The level of communication between the audit team and the client was also rated as very important by all three groups. Audit partner tenure, on the other hand, had a relatively low importance.

Our interview and correspondence evidence

Our evidence was collected not as a random or stratified sample but a cross section of the Big Four, investors, analysists, banks, management and all other stakeholders. See Chapter 1. This can be summarized as follows:

Professional investors: Regard size as important (the global reach and experience argument) as well as quality and actual number of top-level audits performed. But not happy.

Non-professional investors: Not *au fait* at the moment.

Investment banks: Only think of Big Four. Extremely unhappy with Big Four though.

Retail banks: Like the Big Four stamp of approval. Think that is a high-quality audit.

Hedge funds and Analysts: Only think of Big Four. Do not rely solely on audited reports.

Short-sellers: Do not rely on audit opinion at all.

Management or Preparers: Only think of Big Four but not particularly happy.

In summary size matters but more importantly the professional user of annual reports only regard the Big Four as a feasible external auditor. It is not just size, the evidence suggest, but also global reach and experience.

Size matters and equates to the Big Four

The board, but management in particular – the chief executive (CEO), the Chief Financial Officer (CFO), the audit committee (AC) and the chair of the audit committee (ACC) – are probably the prime decision makers in the choice of auditors. Occasionally you find shareholders trying to overturn management and the board's chosen auditor, but because of proxy votes by the institutional shareholders they seldom win.[16] However, it creates adverse press comments in the specialist financial press and unwelcome attention, and very rarely share price movement.

So why does size matter so much to directors, ACs, ACCs, CEOs and CFOs? There are two primary reasons the ACCA study found from detailed focus groups and confirmed by our evidence:

1) Larger firms are seen as being able to offer better services across a wider range of industries.
2) The CFOs argued that the Big Four firms carried a level of prestige that was important for investor confidence.

In terms of quality, all other aspects of the audit process were subsumed within the competence equals size equation. The academic empirical evidence, properly evaluated, comes down in favour of higher quality audit is closely correlated with larger size. Our evidence confirms this. The ACCA studies and focus groups confirm this. The reasons can be summarized as:

- Global reach with offices throughout the world;
- More experience with audits from the same industry or sector, and issues arising therefrom;
- Knowledge of and experience with rare accounting, standards or reporting issues and new standards and regulations;
- Global recognition and prestige of brandname which is recognized by shareholders and other stakeholders;
- All the Big Four have spent massively on technology in recent years and for smaller companies to have access to the same technology is difficult and a weakness.

So whatever happens in the future, size matters and will militate towards the largest of the auditing firms. It also seems that we found some evidence (collected in interviews) that the customers often like to ask their auditors to help with other areas. So an in-depth set of consultancy services was liked before the ARD (the EU's Audit Reform Directive) and the imposition of a) compulsory rotation, b) 70% cap of non-audit fees and c) the blacklists (the list of activities that auditors are not now allowed to undertake). This brings us to our first quality axiom.

Quality axiom 1: size is important and is linked with higher quality audits.

So whatever actions to reform the audit market are undertaken, size will always be important as will prestige.

Notes

1 When the Big Six (including GT and BDO) met recently with the CMA and at the ICAEW, a competition lawyer was present to guard against unintentional collusion.
2 This data was gathered by the authors using third-party, multiple references on social media and recruitment agencies.
3 Both references are from page 83 Gow, I. D., and Kells, S., *The Big Four: The Curious Past and Perilous Future of the Global Accounting Monopoly*, La Trobe University Press, Carlton, Australia, 2018. p. 210 Available at: www.amazon.co.uk/dp/B077YCTV92/ref=dp-kindle-redirect?_encoding=UTF8&btkr=1 Accessed July 2018.
4 Ibid., p. 83.
5 In the UK, a smaller number of Deloitte Haskins & Sells member firms rejected the merger with Touche Ross and shortly thereafter merged with Coopers & Lybrand to form Coopers & Lybrand Deloitte (later to merge with Price Waterhouse to become PwC). Some member firms of Touche Ross also rejected the merger with Deloitte Haskins & Sells and merged with other firms. Touche Ross & Co changed its UK name to Deloitte & Touche from 1 February 1996. Although the UK firm of Deloitte Haskins & Sells had merged with Coopers & Lybrand in 1990 to form Coopers & Lybrand Deloitte, in most of the rest of the world Deloitte Haskins & Sells merged with Touche Ross & Co. Coopers & Lybrand Deloitte dropped the Deloitte in June 1992. The UK offices of Arthur Andersen amalgamated with Deloitte & Touche on 1 August 2002; the new firm practising under the latter name Deloitte & Touche adopted the brandname Deloitte from 1 October 2003.
6 Donnithorne, A., 2018, 'Big Four "break in" young auditors with long hours', *Financial Times*, 16 March 2018. Available at: www.ft.com/content/cc6159f2-284b-11e8-b27e-cc62a39d57a0 Accessed April 2018.
7 Jones, H., 2018, 'Big Four accountants counting on capped market share to avoid break-up', *Reuters*, 1 June 2018. Available at: www.reuters.com/article/britain-accounts-regulator/big-four-accountants-counting-on-capped-market-share-to-avoid-break-up-idUSL8N1TH349 Accessed July 2018.

8   Hosking, P., 2018, 'Grant Thornton gives up battle with Big Four', *The Sunday Times*, 30 March 2018. Available at: www.thetimes.co.uk/article/grant-thornton-gives-up-battle-with-big-four-psvmqbvt0 Accessed April 2018.

9   Marriage, M., 2018, 'Grant Thornton exits audit market for big UK companies', *Financial Times*, 29 March 2018. Available at: www.ft.com/content/c7f1036c-326f-11e8-b5bf-23cb17fd1498 Accessed April 2018.

10 Fino, J., 2018, 'Accountancy firms dominate UK consulting market', *Economia*, March 2018 Quotes taken from Economia and reproduced with kind permission of ICAEW. https://economia.icaew.com/. © ICAEW 2018. Available at: https://economia.icaew.com/en/news/march-2018/accountancy-firms-dominate-uk-consulting-market Accessed April 2018.

11 Consultancy UK, 2018, Available at: www.consultancy.uk/consulting-industry/united-kingdom Accessed January 2018.

12 Berry Dunn (US Accounting firm), 2018, 'Why audit quality matters', Available at: www.berrydunn.com/news-detail/insight-e-news-september-2011-why-audit-quality-matters Accessed April 2018.

13 Deloitte, 2018, 'What is a high quality audit?' Article written by Arta Limani, Senior Manager and Arian Meta, Manager of Deloitte Kosova, published by Amcham's magazine HORIZON. Available at: https://www2.deloitte.com/al/en/pages/audit/articles/high-quality-audit.html Accessed April 2018.

14 DeAngelo, L. E., 1981, 'Auditor size and audit quality', *Journal of Accounting and Economics*, Vol. 3, No. 3, December 1981, pp. 183–199. Available at: www.sciencedirect.com/journal/journal-of-accounting-and-economics/vol/3/issue/3 Accessed May 2018.

15 Fisher, L., 2016, 'The secrets of high-quality audit' ACCA study. *Directors', CFOs' and Auditors' Perceptions of Audit Quality Attributes: A Comparative Study*, carried out with the International Governance and Performance Research Centre (IGAP) at Macquarie University in New South Wales, Australia Summary in the secrets of high-quality audit. Available at: www.accaglobal.com/uk/en/member/member/accounting-business/2016/11-12/insights/audit-secrets.html Accessed May 2018.

16 PSG had a small shareholder revolt over pay and the reappointment of PwC as the auditor. See for example: Crotty, A., 2018, 'PSG to engage with shareholders after hefty opposition to its pay policy', *Business Day*, 25 June 2018. Available at: www.businesslive.co.za/bd/companies/financial-services/2018-06-25-psg-to-engage-with-shareholders-after-hefty-opposition-to-its-pay-policy/ Accessed July 2018. Also BT was preparing for unrest over the appointment and switch to KPMG after negative press reports on the quality of KPMG audits. See for example: Kinder, T., 2018, 'BT prepares for rebellion over KPMG audit switch', *The Times*, 20 June 2018. Available at: www.thetimes.co.uk/article/bt-prepares-for-rebellion-over-kpmg-audit-switch-bvpxc3l0h Accessed July 2018.

4 Disruption in external auditing

Some concepts and misconceptions

Audit quality and length of audit tenure

One argument often used by members of the Big Four is that the familiarity brought by length of audit tenure allows auditors to better understand the business thus enabling them to find more problems. There is also an argument that there is a steep learning curve during the early years of a new audit. This has been supported by research which shows that auditors who have worked with a company for longer than ten years have a positive effect on financial statements.[1] But there is also contradictory evidence, for example KPMG were the auditors for Carillion for 19 years – all of the company's existence.

The Accounting Review is arguably the most prestigious academic accounting journal globally. It has the strictest global review and referee process. An article published there in 2018 comes to a different conclusion. The data referred to above was based solely on Netherlands data with 147 organizations, examining organization by organization. The data examined the process from the viewpoints of misstatements. They looked at 3,465 misstatements by US companies over 14 years (2002 to 2013). The authors, Singer and Zhang,[2] found that auditors discover misstatements far more quickly within the first three years of an audit appointment, but after ten years, the quality of their audit begins to wane. They argue that if US regulators are looking to mandate auditor rotation, the maximum period of engagement should be set at less than ten years.

Within the first 10 years, a one-year increase in auditor tenure will prolong the misstatement duration by approximately 2.02%. This means that, on average, misstatements are 18.18% longer after

10 years of audit tenure than after one year. Beyond 10 years of auditor tenure, the association between auditor tenure and misstatement is insignificant.

They suggest that this points to a deterioration in audit quality starting early in the auditor–client relationship and reveals a longer audit tenure allows misreporting to accumulate and increase. Their research found "a positive and significant association between audit firm tenure and misstatement magnitude, suggesting that longer audit tenure not only results in less timely detection of misstatements, but also leads to misstatements of large magnitudes".[3]

As there is no recent European or UK data, we cannot draw comparisons. However, our guess is that at first, the audit firm is still finding its way round and is more likely to stumble upon areas that might need more investigation. After ten years, the relationship may become closer and more 'cosy'. We investigate this 'cosiness' later in this chapter. So we can conclude:

Quality axiom 2: higher audit quality is linked to shorter length of audit tenure.

This means that auditor rotation should, in theory, be good for audit quality.

Notably, the US watchdog, the PCAOB, believes that long relationships between auditor and client encourage the development of economic and social ties, which in turn undermine auditor independence and audit quality. However, the Republican-led US House of Representatives voted overwhelmingly in 2018 in favour of a bill that blocks the US auditing watchdog from implementing a proposal for mandatory rotation of auditors.[4]

Audit the effect of naming engagement partners on audit quality

The audit engagement, or lead audit partner has been named for some years in the UK. The name is on the audit report itself. There has been some research which shows some correlation between relative share performance and the personal name of the auditor.

The US is just playing catch up from 2017:[5]

Under the new PCAOB rule, which goes into effect on Jan. 31, auditors will be required to file a new PCAOB Form AP, *Auditor*

Reporting of Certain Audit Participants, for each issuer audit, disclosing the following information:

- The name of the engagement partner.
- The names, locations, and extent of participation of other accounting firms that took part in the audit, if their work constituted 5 percent or more of the total audit hours.
- The number and aggregate extent of participation of all other accounting firms that took part in the audit whose individual participation was less than 5 percent of the total audit hours.

The 'Effect of Networked Clients' Economic Importance on Audit Quality'[6] explores the effect of engagement partners on audit quality. The authors contend that the new regulation will clearly help investors recognize situations ripe for auditor conflict of interest. Those conflicts are most likely to happen when a member of a client's audit committee serves in the same function in at least one other company that happens to be a client of the engagement partner – what the study calls "interlock networks".

Our own evidence suggests that the naming of partner on the independent audit report in annual accounts has a significant impact.

Interview and correspondence evidence

As we explained in Chapter 1, we collected extensive interview and correspondence evidence. These are our summaries in the same format as Chapter 3. There is a little overlap, but this summary is more geared towards an overview of what the constituents think of the auditors in general.

Professional investors: Not happy with auditing. Some put it more strongly and less politely.

Auditors: Increasingly worried about changing regulations, FRC's AIC (audit inspection unit) and increasing FRC examination of senior Big Four colleagues, including promotions and salary/benefit levels and any increase of the same. There was also more tension between the audit engagement partner, the chair of the audit committee (ACC) and the audit committee (AC). Both management and auditors did not want to raise the wrath of the FRC.

Big Four specifically: Think they are doing a good job and trying to keep pace with the new regulations. An active set believe a holistic approach is better than a box-ticking approach which the FRC is currently leading them to.

Mid-tier (BDO, GT and the next 20 or so): Less concerned with the more complex auditing. Still do simpler auditing for the FTSE small cap[7] and some AIM firms as well as some internal audit and internal controls.

Smaller practice: Audit is no longer their concern.

Non-professional investors: Found it hard to keep up with all the changes and latest developments. Their expectations of what the auditors should do and what they are actually doing is now the widest it ever has been.

Investment banks: Vary from not at all happy to very actively against the current auditing process.

Retail banks: Do rely on audit opinion and are happy in so far as they are involved.

Commercial banks: Neutral.

Analysts: Not at all happy.

Hedge funds: Do not rely on audited statements.

FRC up to 2016 only: Happy and think they are on the right track. As defined by them, audit quality is improving including the Big Four audits based in the FRC's criteria up to 2017. However, the failures of 2018 changed their views.

Short-sellers: Do not rely on audit opinion at all.

Management and preparers: Not happy. Their problem is too much work. Audit rotation, expanding reports and new regulations all cause more work. Audits seem to be getting increasingly tough. Quite a high proportion rely on information transferred to spreadsheets, rather than from their financial systems. Hence manual errors can arise as in the case of Conviviality (see *Financial Failures and Corporate Scandals: From Enron to Carillion*).

External auditing and the criticisms: a developing story

After the collapse of Carillion in 2018, the Select Committee described the FRC as "useless", while the Big Four and 'City' advisers were accused of "feasting on the carcass" of the failing. Of course, these are easy targets compared to the Carillion directors.

The CMA are now investigating the Big Four with the aim of increasing competition. They argue that breaking up the Big Four or spinning off the firms' audit arms would bring an end to the 'cosy relationships' the firms appear to have with their audit clients, reduce conflicts of interest and drive up audit quality. It would also widen access to the audit marketplace at the higher end, and create greater competition. The FRC also want a say in all senior appointments of the Big Six (add GT and BDO to the Big Four of PwC, Deloitte, KPMG and EY). The FRC has announced that it will use tougher sanctions on the Big Four, likely to be continued and enhanced by the FRC's replacement:

1) £10m fines for seriously poor audit work (the first case was with PwC and BHS of a £10m fine though this was reduced to £8.5m for fast settlement);
2) greater use of non-financial penalties – the most notable being a minimum ten-year ban from the accountancy profession for dishonesty;
3) a say in the top appointments;
4) a new Audit Quality Thematic Review on Materiality (December 2017);[8]
5) an Audit Culture Thematic Review (May 2018)[9] with the intention of creating in audit firms' activities to establish, promote and embed a culture that is committed to delivering consistently high-quality audits;
6) the Audit Quality Review of June 2018,[10] which reported on a decline in audit quality of the Big Four.

As the Big Four audit nearly all the FTSE 350, the argument hinges on:

1) increasing competition by breaking the stranglehold the Big Four has over the audits of the FTSE 350. That was what the Competition Commission's report (in 2012/2013) and the ARD tried to do, but failed. Their combined actions and the increased complexity of an audit and the increased the costs of tendering and running an audit tender makes it less profitable for anyone other than Big Four to tender. The prospect of possible FRC fines may also become an inhibiting factor.
2) reducing the closeness between management of the entity and the auditors; and stopping firms subsidising their audit work with more profitable consultancy work.

It isn't often that the words *hubris, nemesis, insouciance, calamitous failure* and *cartel* are quoted in any article or book concerning the current status quo of the Big Four. But these are criticisms being levelled (see Brooks, 2018).[11] So we return to the theme of 'something's gotta give'[12] as the status quo is no longer tenable.

Audit margins and audit fee increases

Based on interviews with several senior partners of the Big Four, the following is typical of the general feeling:

> I believe the Big Four see audit as very competitive and as a narrow margin area, whilst consultancy, using more experienced staff (perhaps who trained with the firm), is where the big profits are made.

And

> unfortunately, audit work is a lower margin function than our other non-audit work.

In our interviews with partners in the Big Four, it became clear that all the firms priced audit work with lower margins than consultancy. In terms of contribution to profits, it's not clear to us whether some of the audit work makes any contribution, and in some cases might even make a negative contribution, i.e. is subsidized by the consultancy divisions. This probably depends on the (arbitrary) allocation of overheads.

So why is audit so important to these firms? It's difficult to say with any certainty, but we found an ingrained work ethic for audit in all the Big Four. Although it's not the largest profit contributor, most partners in the Big Four regard audit work as a must – to use a cliché, it's part of the firms' DNA. But if one of the Big Four drops out of the audit market, we think that would create a virtual monopoly for tendering. (We discuss this later based on evidence from one managing partner.) This would create an environment for audit fees to rise, especially as the audit scope is likely to increase over time. Such rises may very well be in double digit percentage increases over time.

Evidence of audit fees increasing

Examining the total audit fees for the FTSE 100, audit fees fell initially between 2015/2016 from the prior year by −0.7%. But in the second year of switching, the audit firms were able to increase their audit fees significantly – the largest being Sainsbury with a 143% increase. In general the average increase was 9.4%. See Table 4.1. And we expect this second year increase to be the same amount in subsequent years. Not just for switching firms but all firms – the top 75 firms increased their audit fees by an average of 9.3% in the equivalent period.

Table 4.1 Second year auditor fee comparison (£000s)[13]

Company	New auditor	Audit fees 16/17	Audit fees 15/16	Audit fees 14/15	Audit fees % change 16/17 over 15/16	Audit fees % change 15/16 over 14/15	Audit tenure	Previous auditor
Antofagasta	PwC	913	910	704	0.3%	29.3%	2015	Deloitte
BAT	KPMG	9,200	8,700	9,200	5.7%	−5.4%	2015	PwC
DCC	KPMG	2,229	1,730	1,607	28.8%	7.7%	2016	PwC
Diageo	PwC	6,500	5,700	6,300	14.0%	−9.5%	2016	KPMG
G4S	PwC	8,000	6,000	6,000	33.3%	0.0%	2015	KPMG
HSBC Hldgs	PwC	48,667	45,926	30,526	6.0%	50.4%	2015	KPMG
Sage Group	EY	3,300	2,700	2,000	22.2%	35.0%	2015	PwC
Sainsbury (J)	EY	1,700	700	1,000	142.9%	−30.0%	2016	PwC
Smith & Nephew	KPMG	2,963	2,963	2,256	0.0%	31.3%	2015	EY
Tesco	Deloitte	5,500	5,900	4,600	−6.8%	28.3%	2016	PwC
Whitbread	Deloitte	800	800	600	0.0%	33.3%	2016	EY
Total		89,771	82,029	64,793	9.4%	26.6%		
FTSE 100		85,583	86,173		−0.7%			

The practice of raising the fee in the second year after tendering is becoming endemic. Of the FTSE 250 (the next largest 250 companies after the FTSE 100), second year fee income rose by an average of 24%. *Accountancy Magazine's*[14] annual survey identified:

> A trend first highlighted a year ago of fee increases for the second year of an audit has been confirmed in this year's survey – while fees actually fell by 7% in the first year after the audit changed hands, there was a 24% increase for those audits that were in their second year with a new audit firm. Some of this increase could be put down to corporate activity, such as mergers and acquisitions, but it seems that following the first year, auditors are going back to their audit committee bosses to ask for more fees, often changing the scope of the audit in the process.

Stephen Griggs, head of audit at Deloitte agrees:

> When the regulations were first introduced, audit tendering was a hot topic and a number of companies went out to tender early. The

current round of tendering has now largely played out in the FTSE 100. The FTSE 250 companies, which are perhaps not as high profile as their FTSE 100 counterparts, are typically letting the regulatory timetable unfold. As a consequence, tendering is actually more orderly in the run-up to 2023.[15]

The role of the auditor and what the statutory audit does not do

Irrespective of definitions, what the professional investors, the employees and the suppliers want from the auditor is some sort of assurance that a company can continue or that management is making effective decisions. As the KPMG letter[16] defending Carillion's external audit shows, this is not what the auditors believe they are doing in general (we accept that Carillion may be an extreme case and errors of judgement could have been made). But it is what the stakeholders demand. Herein lies the expectations gap and a clash of opinions and function. Something has to give.

Auditors rely on guidance from the FRC to define what their duties should be. This is not particularly helpful given that its guidance on going concern (up to 12 months) concludes (now being strengthened):

> on the appropriateness of the directors' use of the going concern basis of accounting and, based on the audit evidence obtained, whether a material uncertainty exists related to events or conditions . . . may cast significant doubt on the entity's (or where relevant, the group's) ability to continue as a going concern. If the auditor concludes that a material uncertainty exists, the auditor is required to draw attention in the auditor's report to the related disclosures in the financial statements or, if such disclosures are inadequate, to modify the auditor's opinion. The auditor's conclusions are based on the audit evidence obtained up to the date of the auditor's report. However, future events or conditions may cause the entity (or where relevant, the group) to cease to continue as a going concern.[17]

You can tell that this statement was written by an auditor and that may be one of the criticisms of the FRC. This definition is woolly and opaque and provides an auditor with a range of meanings. KPMG took the narrowest interpretation. Some auditors might take a wider and more encompassing view. Then there is the auditors' responsibility with the longer-term (more than 12 months) viability statement. All this may change over the next few years. The new set of governance codes[18] empowers shareholders and other stakeholders, and emphasizes changes to board composition and remunerations. Apart from this, in our view the new governance code is rather lame given the press comments leading up to its release. However, there will be other recommendations, with more teeth, that may arise post-Carillion, both out of the review of the FRC, and the referral to the competition watchdog.

Disruption and rotation of the external auditing process

What determines the winning formula for an audit tender?

This section draws upon interviews and various documents provided by the Big Four,[19] our own research and survey data, several confidential articles and several unpublished PhD theses.[20] The most important conclusion is that the personal relationships of the lead auditor partner and his or her team are probably the biggest influence in deciding who wins the audit tender.

The overlap period between an auditor going and the new auditor taking over is usually around two to three years. The problem for the incumbent auditor is that any suggestion they might make will likely meet the retort, "Why didn't you raise this before?". So the incumbent starts at a disadvantage. The newcomer can make positive or new suggestions which means that once at the tender stage, there is an element of 'the grass is greener' which encourages a tendency to switch. Although the incumbent may have knowledge and understanding, this may bring complacency. The incumbent does have the advantage that there is a great deal of hassle in changing auditors, but conversely management changes may make the incumbent's position less comfortable.

Pre-audit services and targeting activities

One aspect of winning a tender is the targeting of particular services outside the official audit. These activities include technical accounting updates provided by a firm to company personnel, secondments of firm staff to the company before the tender process, introducing company management to relevant contacts from within the firms (for example contacts in critical territories) and so on. Offering non-audit work can be used as a method of gaining a measure of closeness before the audit tender. Another positive factor is past experience of one or more of the directors with the audit firm. Non-professional social relationships did not seem to factor.

In general, the auditor tendering process between the Big Four and GT/BDO is remarkably similar. There does seem to be a degree of tailoring with specific proposals which formed part of the final proposal for tendering. The most important of these is the working relationship between the auditors and the company being audited.

Box 4.1   Factors taken into consideration in the audit tendering process

Working relationships

People talked about the importance of identifying people they could work with (as an objective of the future audit service).

Accounting technical matters

These were also taken into account as an area for consideration in auditor selection.

Coordination and communication

The importance of audit issue management to auditor selection was identified in several interviews. Companies wanted to know that issues would be appropriately escalated from divisional audits, but also that unnecessary alerts which were not really substantive audit issues were avoided. There was some concern that issues may be raised which, when discussed and thought through with the auditor, turned out not to be important.

IT systems and controls

Some tenders relied too much on IT for some companies. Other liked this approach.

Working with internal audit

This was also an area that was considered.

Price was very rarely important. Fees were found generally not to be a major influence on auditor appointment. This was either because the fee quotes were close, or because companies felt the fees were unimportant as they represent a small proportion of total spend, or because negotiations took place after the decision or as part of the decision with the preferred bidder. Lead partners were often in discussions about the negotiations over fees once close to being chosen.

Capabilities and competences

Under the heading of capabilities and competences, the firm being audited wanted to know about the team and the lead partner, and how the team was structured. Behavioural influences focussed on interactions between the audit teams and the companies including (even most importantly) the existence of personal chemistry. Audit partners felt that informality and discussion was critical to establishing this chemistry. Effort, enthusiasm and responsiveness were also important. For many, the final presentation was important.

In the majority of cases, decisions were close but the final discussion was consensual between the selection panels, which included both non-executives and executives. Audit committee chairs were involved but there was also an influential role for management, especially the finance director. Sometimes it was the chief executive and the finance director that made the final decision. Several companies felt that they could dismiss one of the audit firms fairly quickly and easily, usually due to a personality factor.

Disruption and implications of the tendering process

In conclusion, it seems that the most important aspect of the tendering process is the ability of the audit teams and lead partner (or two partners in some cases) to establish a personal relationship and a good rapport with the client. These relationships depend on the personnel involved, which militates towards sociable and personable audit staff who can establish good working relationships, over and above pure technical expertise. This is especially true of the lead partner. Not everyone in the audit firm is going to 'get on' with everyone in the company being audited. The chief executive, finance director and chair of the audit committee seemed to be the most influential personnel in the tendering process – especially where the tenders were close (and they often were).

The constraints are the core audit and service design, the ability to have had one's foot in the door previously by some non-audit work or specific projects and core capabilities and competences including relevant experience. These factors tend to encourage gravitation towards the Big Four.

The problem with the tendering process is that it brings the closeness of the relationship between the company being audited and the auditors to the fore: 'You will not win an audit unless there is personal chemistry' seems to be the mantra. So how does this correlate with independence and a healthy and necessary dose of scepticism? A new audit team will take time (often more than a year) to get to know and understand a large company being audited. Scepticism has to be learnt alongside knowledge and understanding of the firm being audited which usually takes considerably longer than a year or even two.

Notes

1 A summary of this article can be found in Van Burren, J., and Paape, L., 2012, 'The longer the audit tenure the better says Dutch research', *Accountancy Age*, 2018. Available at: www.accountancyage.com/aa/feature/2170375/audit-tenures-positively-affects-businesses Accessed April 2018.

2 Zvi, S., and Jing, Z., 2018, 'Auditor tenure and the timeliness of misstatement discovery', *The Accounting Review*, Vol. 93, No. 2, March 2018, pp. 315–338. Available at: http://aaapubs.org/doi/abs/10.2308/accr-51871 Accessed April 2018. Also see recent research, published in later editions of *The Accounting Review*. Available at: http://aaapubs.org/loi/accr

3 See for example: Irvine, J., 2018, 'Audit quality benefits from short audit tenure', *Economia*, 6 April 2018. Quotes taken from *Economia* and reproduced with kind permission of ICAEW. https://economia.icaew.com/. © ICAEW 2018. Available at: https://economia.icaew.com/en/news/april-2018/audit-quality-benefits-from-short-audit-tenure Accessed April 2018.

4 Irvine, J., 2018, 'US blocks mandatory auditor rotation', *Economia*, 9 July 2013. Quotes taken from *Economia* and reproduced with kind permission of ICAEW. https://economia.icaew.com/. © ICAEW 2013. Available at: https://economia. icaew.com/news/july2013/us-blocks-mandatory-auditor-rotation Accessed April 2017.

5 Sheridan, T., 2016, 'Why new PCAOB rule should improve audit quality', *Accounting Web*, 28 December 2016. Available at: www.accountingweb.com/aa/auditing/why-new-pcaob-rule-should-improve-audit-quality Accessed April 2018.

6 Hossain, S., Monroe, G., S., Wilson, M., and Jubb, M., 2016, 'The effect of networked clients' economic importance on audit quality', *AUDITING: A Journal of Practice & Theory*, Vol. 35, No. 4, November 2016, pp. 79–103. Available at: www.aaajournals.org/doi/abs/10.2308/ajpt-51451?code=aaan-site Accessed April 2018.

7 Listed but below the FTSE 350 often called FTSE small caps.

8 Financial Reporting Council, 2017, 'Audit quality thematic review: Materiality', *Financial Reporting Council*, December 2017. Available at: www.frc.org.uk/getattachment/4713123b-919c-4ed6-a7a4-869aa9a668f4/Audit-Quality-Thematic-Review-Materiality-(December-2017).pdf Accessed April 2018.

9 Financial Reporting Council, 2018, 'Audit culture thematic review: Firms' activities to establish, promote and embed a culture that is committed to delivering consistently high quality audits', *Financial Reporting Council*, May 2018. Available at: www.frc.org.uk/getattachment/2f8d6070-e41b-4576-9905-4aeb7df8dd7e/Audit-Culture-Thematic-Review.pdf Accessed June 2018.

10 Financial Reporting Council News, 'Big Four Audit Quality Review results decline', *Financial Reporting Council*, 18 June 2018. Available at: www.frc.org.uk/news/june-2018/big-four-audit-quality-review-results-decline Accessed July 2018.

11 Books, R., 2018, 'The financial scandal no one is talking about: Accountancy used to be boring – and safe. But today it's neither. Have the "big four" firms become too cosy with the system they're supposed to be keeping in check?', *The Guardian*, 29 May 2018. Available at: www.theguardian.com/news/2018/may/29/the-financial-scandal-no-one-is-talking-about-big-four-accountancy-firms Accessed June 2018. See also: Brooks, R., *Bean Counters: The Triumph of the Accountants and How They Broke Capitalism*, Atlantic Books, 2018. Theme runs throughout the book.

12 *Something's Gotta Give* is a 2003 romantic comedy film written, starring Jack Nicholson and Diane Keaton as a successful 60-something and 50-something, who find love for each other in later life, despite being complete opposites. See: https://en.wikipedia.org/wiki/Something%27s_Gotta_Give_(film)

13 Based on but modified from figures produced in *Accountancy Magazine*.

14 We are extremely fortunate to have this must-have source which is essential to understanding the accountancy profession. Smith, P., 2018, 'FTSE 250 Auditors Survey 2018: Turning up the heat on audit firms', *Accountancy Daily/Magazine*, 31 May 2018. Available at: www.accountancydaily.co/ftse-250-auditors-survey-2018-turning-heat-audit-firms Accessed June 2018. And Smith, P., 2017, 'FTSE 100 Auditors Survey 2017', *Accountancy Daily/Magazine*, 1 November 2017. Available at: www.accountancydaily.co/ftse-100-auditors-survey-2017 Accessed April 2018.

15 Ibid.

16 Letter from KPMG to the Chairs, 2 February 2018. This was in connection with: House of Commons. *Business, Energy and Industrial Strategy and Work and Pensions Committees*. Carillion. Second Joint report from the Business, Energy and Industrial Strategy and Work and Pensions Committees of Session 2017–19. HC 769. Letter is available on: www.parliament.uk/documents/commons-committees/work-and-pensions/Correspondence/Letter-from-KPMG-Chairman-to-the-Chairs-relating-to-Carillion-2-February-2018.pdf Accessed March 2018.

17 Financial Reporting Council, 2016, 'Description of the auditor's responsibilities for the audit of the financial statements', *Financial Reporting Council*, 17 June 2016. Available at: www.frc.org.uk/auditors/audit-assurance/auditor-s-responsibilities-for-the-audit-of-the-fi/description-of-the-auditor%E2%80%99s-responsibilities-for Accessed July 2016. Also see the new recommendation: https://www.frc.org.uk/news/march-2019/frc-consults-on-stronger-going-concern-standard-fo

18 Financial Reporting Council News, 2018, 'A UK Corporate Governance Code that is fit for the future', *Financial Reporting Council*, 16 July 2018. Available at: www.frc.org.uk/news/july-2018/a-uk-corporate-governance-code-that-is-fit-for-the Accessed July 2018. This page leads to a number of relevant documents: 'The UK corporate governance code', July 2018. Available at: www.frc.org.uk/getattachment/88bd8c45-50ea-4841-95b0-d2f4f48069a2/2018-UK-Corporate-Governance-Code-FINAL.pdf; 'Revised UK corporate governance code 2018 highlights'. Available at: www.frc.org.uk/getattachment/524d4f4b-62df-4c76-926a-66e223ca0893/2018-UK-Corporate-Governance-Code-high lights.pdf; 'Guidance on board effectiveness', July 2018. Available at: www.frc.org.uk/document-library/corporate-governance/2018/guidance-on-board-effectiveness. This link does not open a page but just downloads this report. And the consultation document: 'The Wates corporate governance principles for large private companies', *Financial Reporting Council*, 13 June 2018. Available at: www.frc.org.uk/consultation-list/2018/consultation-the-wates-corporate-govern

ance-princ. To download this report: www.frc.org.uk/getattachment/48653f86-92c3-4cd6-8465-da4b7cac0034/;.aspx

19 Including several PhD theses (to remain anonymous) and interviews.

20 Much of this material is confidential or awaiting publication. One influential thesis was: 'The factors affecting the auditor selection decisions of FTSE 350 companies in competitive tenders'. PhD thesis by Philp Drew, 2015. School of Management, Cranfield University.

5 Disputes in external auditing

Disruption in auditing

The audit industry matters. It is an important safeguard and external check without which much less confidence would be placed in our listed companies. It is also in those companies' interest – if investors cannot trust financial statements, then the companies' cost of capital will rise, crippling growth and threatening employment.

Competition (as measured by number of firms) and audit quality

We measure competition by the number of firms competing. Recent studies are scarce in the UK or US as the audit market has been dominated by the Big Four. There are concerns whether the lack of competition in the audit market may reduce audit quality.

Existing research provides conflicting empirical results on whether competition directly reduces audit quality, though later research is more decisive. There are many articles and we cannot mention them all here. Kallapur (2008)[1] found that higher audit market competition is associated with lower audit quality. This was confirmed by Newton et al. (2013)[2] where lower audit market competition led to fewer restatements. Velte (2012)[3] did not disprove the above but found that EU reforms cannot clearly be related to increase audit quality but increasing transaction costs.

Xie (2016),[4][5] using US data and innovative modelling techniques, found the reverse – that increased competition increased audit quality, and that greater audit market competition significantly increases audit quality. Other recent studies confirm these conclusions. Based on our trawl though the academic studies, our evaluation favoured the proposition that greater competition is correlated with higher quality audits.

Audit quality a function of competition and exogenous variables

We did not perform the same sort of tests used in the academic research above. What we did was to canvass opinions on the subject. We found that there is an entrenched feeling that audit quality can improve with greater competition. However, evidence collected during 2013 to 2015 was more mixed. Evidence collected during 2016 and 2017 argued much more strongly for more competition. We think that this slight change in view was due to the more complex and uncertain environment. It can be argued that new regulations, combined with a rapidly changing environment and an uncertain future, might play havoc with audit quality. Given these conditions, and based on our evidence, we conclude that the lack of competition does not help audit quality.

What we also contend is that audit quality is a function of changing regulations and the degree of change, disruption, complexity and exogenous shocks to economic, regulatory and business environments. Brexit and technology may have had a significant impact. Hold everything constant and audit quality seems less affected by competition (or the number of audit firms competing in the audit market). Put the two concepts together and the strength of the positive relationship between audit quality and greater competition is influenced by many external factors but especially turbulent economic environment.

Hence:

Quality axiom 3: greater competition leads to better audit quality. An increase in the number of firms competing leads to higher audit quality. In periods of turbulence and disruption this relationship is strengthened.

The CMA offer some articles disproving this. However, we have provided a strong criticism of their conclusions and some additional references supporting our conclusions. See http://www.fin-rep.org/wp-content/uploads/book2/5-Our-response-to-the-CMA-update-paper.pdf

The debate over the FRC's role

A word of caution here. There is some dispute whether the personal views of Stephen Haddrill, the former chief executive of the FRC, and the FRC's official views differ. Several people within the Big Four were not quite sure what the position of the FRC is. Mr Haddrill may not personally reflect the publicly adopted position and press releases of the FRC. Though it seems from recent releases that those views seemed to have prevailed and in its more recent statements, the FRC seems to have adopted its CEOs position. Disruption always causes a bit of chaos . . .

FRC and the Kingman Review

The FRC also responded positively to the announcement of the Kingman Review (now completed):

> The review provides an opportunity to consider changing public expectations and whether our powers are adequate to meet those.[6]

The Sir John Kingman Review is limited to just the FRC – with the aim to make the FRC the best in class for corporate governance and transparency.[7]

The Kingman report has been accepted by the Government in March 2019. The review recommends that the FRC be replaced with an independent statutory regulator called the Audit, Reporting and Governance Authority (ARGA). Many of the criticism below was voiced in the Kingman review and may be eliminated by the new ARGA.

Criticisms of the FRC

The FRC has long been viewed as a 'soft touch', 'toothless' and 'chronically passive' having let KPMG off the hook over its auditing of HBOS, closing an investigation into PwC's failure to spot that Barclays had put £16.5 billion of client assets at risk, ditto with Tesco, and doing nothing with MG Rover.[8]

The full list of complaints against the FRC include:[9]

* Too often does not implement any sanctions despite evidence of wrongdoing;
* In general has had too 'light a touch' and fails to be tough enough in its sanctions;
* Lacks clarity around the FRC's purpose;
* Lacks adequate powers (it regulates auditors, accountants and actuaries, not directors);
* Has failed to ensure that the industry learns from its mistakes;
* Is too close to the Big Four; too many staff drawn from the Big Four;
* Drags its feet or takes too long over investigations.

Box 5.1   The Kingman Review – Independent Review of the Financial Reporting Council – Call for Evidence[10]

* FRC purpose and function;
* Impact and effectiveness;
* Audit regulation;

- Accounting and financial reporting;
- Corporate Governance and Stewardship Codes;
- Speed and effectiveness of investigations; enforcement and compliance;
- Actuarial oversight;
- FRC and corporate failure;
- Powers and sanctions;
- The FRC's legal status and its relationship with government;
- Governance and leadership;
- Funding, resources and staffing.

The report, now published, is discussed in www.fin-rep.org

Though the Kingman Review categorizes such complaints under its scheme shown in Box 5.1, the FRC would argue that it is primarily constrained by resources. Their cases are complex, sometimes involving millions of documents, and they are often extensively challenged by independent tribunals or judicial reviews. All these cases are examined in detail in the *Financial Failures and Corporate Scandals: From Enron to Carillion* volume in this series which examines in depth the cases of Carillion, Conviviality, Sig, Autonomy amongst others.

The Kingman Review was effective and scrapped the FRC in favour of ARGA with statutory powers making it a stronger regulator with harsher penalties and the ability to investigate all company directors. ARGA will also be able to make changes to accounts, have a wider set of sanctions and can publish reports into a company's conduct and management. The Government has said it would implement the Review.

The failure of Carillion in 2018 elicited a plethora of criticisms of the FRC from a cross section of sources and subsequently the Kingman Review was announced. The feeling is that this spurred the FRC into action. Looking at its publications, actions and investigations, the FRC certainly appeared much more proactive from Spring 2018. The *Sunday Times* headline[11] was:

> FRC: the watchdog that barked too late. After a string of corporate collapses, has the accounting regulator finally found its teeth?

The same article explained:

> The accountancy boss did not hide his disdain. "It's reacting like a caged animal", he said of his industry's regulator, the FRC. "The chained-up dog, after being prodded with a stick, is now thrashing around."

Naturally, the FRC denied that Kingman Review or Carillion spurred it into action.

The FT mentioned two failures (in addition to Carillion) that the paper feels were significant:[12]

> Last year, the FRC cleared the accounting firm KPMG of any wrongdoing during its audit of defunct lender HBOS, which collapsed during the financial crisis. The verdict, and the fact that it took nearly a decade to open an investigation into KPMG, raised questions about the willingness of the FRC to take action against accountancy firms.
>
> The concerns were amplified after the FRC decided to clear PwC, another of the "big four" accounting firms, of any wrongdoing while working for Barclays, despite the bank being fined a record £37.7m in 2014 for failing to keep client money separate from its own.

Economia reported:

> Tim Bush, head of governance and financial analysis at PIRC [Pensions & Investment Research Consultants] and a long time campaigner against the FRC, welcomed the move. "The FRC has failed to use the tools already available to it", he said. "Mistranscription of the law is one example. There is clear evidence that the FRC has owed more to defence − of poor accounts and audit − than attack. A classic creature of regulatory capture."[13]

FRC's lack of clarity

In our view the role of the FRC has evolved. There are two remaining gaps (both perhaps filled by the Kingman report):

- Preparer-accountant. The FRC should be able to prove breach of a rule rather than behaviour amounting to misconduct.
- Preparer-directors[14] who are not accountants. There is no sanction that the FRC can impose currently − though we suspect the Kingman Review will recommend closing that gap. They have fallen through the cracks unless the FCA picks them up (but it cannot touch private companies). The Kingman report in its specification for the FRC replacement (ARGA) supports sanctions but still leaves disqualification with the Insolvency service.

The criticism of 'lacking clarity of purpose' may be just a reaction to the evolution of the FRC informed by changing EU regulation and directives, and the decisions of political masters. Certainly, then Prime Minister Theresa May has heavily criticized big business although press reports indicate that she may have calmed her views:

> Theresa May's great crusade against big business fat-cats has lapsed into minor tinkering: the idea of installing Swedish-style shareholder committees to approve directors and oversee pay is mentioned but not prominently, implying it won't happen.[15]

FRC's organizational structure

One of the issues raised is that the FRC is judge, jury and executioner on all matters of reporting, accounting and auditing.

> It sets standards, it investigates and it punishes. It doesn't feel right to us that all the power is in one place.[16]

Note the Kingman report recommends even more teeth for the ARGA (FRC's replacement).

The *Sunday Times* also aptly described this as:

> Accountants, admittedly speaking from self-interest, argue that the FRC has become overly focused on the cane, at the expense of schooling, but critics of the FRC say it does not even do that – it simply doles out punishments, rather than proposing how to fix problems. This leads to the same issues repeating themselves, they say.[17]

Possible recommendations by the Kingman Review are provided in Appendix 1.05.1. Also see updates in http://www.fin-rep.org/which-book/disruption-to-the-audit-market/

The background to the FRC's viewpoint

The audit-only initiative came from the Competition Commission's (CMA's predecessor) look at the auditing sector in 2013, which produced a stricter regime for the auditing sector. Subsequently in 2016 the EU's Audit Reform Directive implemented mandatory rotation, a 70% cap on non-audit fees and a blacklist of work that cannot be conducted. But none of this has increased competition – in fact quite the reverse.

The revolving door

The FT reported on a famous case in the US:

> KPMG fired six US employees over a scandal that calls into question efforts to ensure that public company accounts are being properly scrutinised. Here's what happened: KPMG recruited an employee from the PCAOB, which is charged with overseeing the nearly 2,000 accounting firms that audit US companies. The watchdog inspects the Big Four and other firms annually by taking a random sample of audits and checking them for deficiencies and conflicts of interest. KPMG says that its new employee received a heads up from someone who still worked at the PCAOB about which audits would be inspected. The new employee then shared the information around. Eventually, five partners, including the head of the US audit practice, "either had improper advance warnings" or were aware that others had received this information and "failed to properly report the situation in a timely manner", the firm said. All six people have been fired.[18]

No one is saying that there has been any wrongdoing in the UK, but this is the worry and indeed the FRC has investigated such appointments. (Glyn Barker, mentioned below, is an ex-student of Krish's).

> In September 2013, the FRC announced it was launching an investigation into the audit of the financial statements for the year ended 30 April 2012, as a result of a former PwC partner joining the board of the housing group. The investigation focussed on the appointment of Glyn Barker,[19] who was appointed as non-executive director on 3 January last year. Barker, who had been with PwC for 35 years, had held a number of senior posts including UK vice chairman and head of assurance. Today the regulator said it has been decided that no further action will be taken and the case will be closed.
>
> A PwC spokesperson said, "We cooperated fully with the FRC in its investigation and are pleased that, having investigated the matter, the FRC has closed it without any action."
>
> Shortly after the probe was announced last year Berkeley dropped PwC as auditor in favour of Big Four rival KPMG. PwC audited Berkeley since 1984.[20]

The degree of freedom of choice

Many of the top listed companies employ at least two of the Big Four: one for auditing and one for consulting and advisory work. In the Carillion example, it appears that all four of the Big Four had worked for Carillion in the last ten years. Two were paid consulting fees days before the collapse: PwC's fees were (we would guess) for help with financing and/or sales of assets, and advising the defunct company's pension trustees.[21] EY's fees were cost reduction and a very negative report. So counting KPMG's audit fees, three of the Big Four were being paid. PwC also had a hand in the liquidation process and had some role in advising the government on pensions (not related to Carillion). The lack of choice which Carillion had is similar to the Vodafone example given discussed in Chapter 8 and 9 (see page 96).

There was also the 'cat among the pigeons' effect when GT withdrew from auditing the largest listed companies, after concluding it was too difficult to compete with the market domination of the Big Four firms. This makes it more difficult for the Big Four to argue that there is competition. As one managing partner of the Big Four said in discussing the ARD:

> it effectively creates a situation where the Big Four would win and rotation would be effectively reduced to two – one being the existing auditor and the second being the tax advisor; leaving a choice between just two.

The GT decision to withdraw will deal a blow to efforts by the Big Four to convince politicians and regulators not to intervene in the market. It will also increase pressure on UK authorities to tackle their dominance: as being considered by the CMA and Kingman letter see http://www.fin-rep.org/wp-content/uploads/book2/4-CMA-and-Kingman-reports-update.pdf

The Big Four counter-attack

But the argument goes on. The Big Four counter-attack the FRC by implying it had been too soft:

> Accountancy firms and the FRC have faced growing criticism from Westminster after the collapse of Carillion, BHS and other companies. However, senior figures in the accountancy industry, who have been rattled by the criticism, feel that the credibility of the profession is being undermined by the FRC's weak response to corporate collapses, rather than the dominance of the Big Four.[22]

Perversely this seems to argue for a tougher FRC and yet the same press report goes on to say:

> We are worried they are not seen as strong enough and they fail on regulation. My fear is we end up with a tougher regulator being imposed on the industry [as indeed is the case in the Kingman Review].[23]

There is one quote which explains the angst felt by the Big Four:

> The body [FRC] has drifted into spheres where it lacks the experience – and sometimes the legal authority – to be effective. A partner at a Big Four firm said the FRC was scrutinising senior appointments more, but likened its attempts to widen its remit to "someone who bakes bread suddenly being asked to make a Michelin-starred meal".[24]

So the Big Four's position is that the credibility of the profession is being undermined by the FRC's weak response to corporate collapses, rather than the dominance of the Big Four. The FRC's replacement (ARGA) is likely to be even tougher.

Other viewpoints on the Big Four

The ICAEW viewpoint

The English chartered accountants institute entered the fray with this comment by Michael Izza, their chief executive. His comment is:

> There is a convenient syllogism to which all of us are prone – you may recognise it yourself. It goes "Something must be done. This is something, therefore we must do this." It is perhaps in this light that we are currently hearing more calls to "break up the Big Four".
>
> It's easy to see how we've got here. Everyone agrees there is a problem with market concentration in audit. It's not the elephant in the room, so much as the gorilla in the doorway. Everyone is happy to grumble about the problem, but no one wants to acknowledge that solving it will be very difficult and means we all have to work together – not just in the UK, but in all the markets where these firms operate.
>
> Until now, there has been consensus that the complex, but sustainable, answer to market choice is not to break but to build. . . .
>
> Audit is evolving, and must keep evolving, in order to meet the needs of society. So much good work has been done over the last ten years. Let us not throw it all away just because "something must be done".[25]

He also argues that we should ask "what is putting other large firms off from entering this market?" But we know that size and quality are equated from Chapter 3 so that is not a solution. Mr Izza is also critical of the FRC in that "it now takes several months to review audits, and the disincentive for audit partners to risk their careers as a result of protracted investigations". He also raises the question of unlimited liability and this is evaluated in later chapters. He also wants to remove barriers to entry, another issue discussed in later chapters.

Shape up, not break up: reforming the Big Four

A surprising defence of the Big Four comes from the *Economist* which has often been an ardent critic. For example:

> Investors have exaggerated expectations of auditors' ability to detect fraud. Because audits rely on sampling, some skulduggery will inevitably slip through. There are also signs that the industry is improving. Many countries tightened the rules after a scandal in 2001 sank Enron, an energy-trading firm, and its auditor, Arthur Andersen. In America the number of accounts that are restated because of a material error has fallen sharply over the past decade. Break-up would bring unintended consequences. As the world economy shifts from making goods to selling services, auditing is becoming more complicated: scale and the multidisciplinary expertise of large firms count for more. Smaller firms risk being too reliant on a few large clients, which may cloud their judgment.[26]

Possible solutions and radical fixes are further discussed in later chapters.

Expansion of the Big Four/auditors' responsibilities

The second avenue of the FRC's strategy is that it wants to expand auditors' responsibilities, by requiring them to examine companies' financial reports from "front to back", or the entire report. This policy shift was announced by the FRC's ex-CEO, Stephen Haddrill, in an interview to the ICAEW's (the chartered accountants body) magazine *Economia* (April 2018).[27] There may be or is an internal consultation that would examine work done by auditors, in a bid to increase shareholders' confidence in the auditing process. He said:

> "There are a lot of numbers in the annual report that do not adhere to accounting standards", Haddrill told the Financial Times. "This data can be very useful to investors, but it's not audited and it's not done to a consistent standard. So should that be audited in future? I think there is a case for that, because investors rely on it."

A FRC spokesperson said that the internal review, which is still in the preliminary stages, aims to look at how the auditor is responding to the revised requirements in respect of other information (ISA 720) in the annual report and accounts. Currently, auditors examine the financial statements in companies' annual reports, but do not audit other sections of the report such as directors' reports.

Economia also reported that Nigel Sleigh-Johnson, head of the financial reporting faculty at ICAEW, said,

> It is entirely possible for an auditor to give an opinion over the whole of an annual report. In 2013 we argued that since many people are asking what can be done to make business information more trusted, assurance on the annual report – going beyond the audit of the financial statements – is a vital part of the practical solution to this problem. We continue to believe this.

Of course, there are challenges involved in the development of new assurance services. And we have modelled our view of the audit market and the result is that based on reasonable assumptions this may be more than £20 billion by 2030 to 2035, and not all of this will be fulfilled by the Big Four (if they continue to exist). Any new requirement for an auditor's opinion over the annual report will need to build on an emerging best practice.

Views on independence from the Big Four

Shareholders and professional investors are understandably upset. But one of the triggers of their dissatisfaction was prompted by the FRC's decision in September 2017 to close its investigation into the conduct of KPMG regarding its audit of HBOS's activities in 2007. (HBOS was bought by Lloyds Banking Group in 2008.) The FRC concluded that there was "no realistic prospect" that a disciplinary tribunal would rule that KPMG's audit had fallen "significantly short of the standards reasonably to be expected". Another similar case is Barclays Bank. The FRC cleared PwC over its checks on Barclays. The lender had already been fined £38 million for improperly mixing up client assets with its own money, yet PwC, which had repeatedly signed off on official reports that Barclays was complying with client asset rules, was in effect declared innocent.[28]

The complaints include:

1) The revolving door syndrome: despite efforts since 2011 to rid the FRC of conflicts of interest, it remains excessively dependent on the audit profession for staff funding. Too many of the FRC staff come from the audit profession and in particular the Big Four. (The FRC

disputes this but as of 2018 the number of staff coming from the Big Four was significant.)

2) Piecemeal changes to the FRC's legal basis over the years have left its powers and responsibilities confused, which have been exacerbated by opacity and weak governance structures.[29]

3) The FRC has failed to take actions over many decisions: HBOS, MG Rover, Tesco, Barclays and many others. The usual rhetoric is there is insufficient evidence to make a case.

The actions these professional investors want include:

• Calling for the government to scrap the FRC's current structure and placing it under robust oversight – complaint made in a letter to the government. This in turn follows a similar demand a year ago from consultancy PIRC, which said the FRC should be broken up after it emerged the watchdog had failed to enforce stakeholder reporting provisions in section 172 of the UK's Companies Act 2006.

• Spinning off the FRC's standard-setting function from its enforcement role as part of a wide-ranging reform package.

Taken together, it is our view that the FRC in its current form cannot be relied upon to provide essential scrutiny of the audit profession, and does not act as an effective deterrent to substandard audits and also corporate reporting. The Kingman report agreed.[30]

The cosiness between the Big Four and the FTSE 100 and perhaps the FTSE 350

Accountancy Daily, December 2017, reported this closeness in the relationship having surveyed the FTSE 100:[31]

While the Big Four audit firms continue to totally dominate the FTSE 100 audit market . . . it is easy to forget that their influence extends deep into the boardrooms of these companies as well. Exclusive research by Accountancy reveals that 61 out of the 100 audit committee chair positions in this highest level of corporate UK are held by someone who previously worked for at least one of these firms – Deloitte, EY, KPMG and PwC – or one of their predecessor firms.

Not only that, but a similar proportion (64%) of CFOs are eligible to join one of the Big Four alumni programmes, while a further 15% of board chairs can claim a similar heritage.

Many of these former employees, directors or partners will have left their alma maters some years beforehand to pursue a career in industry. But a significant number would have spent their whole professional careers in just one of the Big Four, perhaps even becoming its senior partner, to then retire and build a portfolio of non-executive positions.

Accountancy's research reveals that 14 FTSE 100 companies are currently audited by a firm where the current audit committee chair also spent part of their career. The equivalent number for CFOs is 13.

One professional investor when confronted with this information said:

> So someone from the Big Four crossing over the management knows exactly what the auditors will look at and what they won't. If they wanted to, it would be easy for the crossing over personnel to help management hide anything from the auditors.

Post publication, the Kingman Review recommended that the FRC be replaced with an independent statutory regulator called ARGA. This new body had many, but not all, of our own recommendations.

The government have accepted the Kingman Review and the new ARGA will replace the FRC. This new regulator will be an independent statutory authority. ARGA should be accountable to Parliament, have clarity of purpose and mission, new leadership, and new powers to keep pace with a changing market with an eye to the prevention of another Carillion. The Kingman Review made 83 basic recommendations – all of which are expected to be adopted by the government. Though for us some of these do not go far enough. That said, it will be much tougher and will have more sanctions over auditors and companies. It will have harsher penalties and the ability to investigate all company directors. ARGA will also be able to make changes to accounts, have a wider set of sanctions and can publish reports into a company's conduct and management.

Notes

1 Kallapur, S., and Sankaraguruswamy, S., 2009, 'Audit market competition and audit quality', *Paper from School of Accountancy*, Singapore Management University, 2009. Available at: http://citeseerx.ist.psu.edu/viewdoc/download?doi=10.1.1.6 28.5104&rep=rep1&type=pdf Accessed April 2017.

2 Newton, J., N., Wang, D., and Wilkins, M., S., 2013, 'Does a lack of choice lead to lower quality? Evidence from auditor competition and client restatements', *Auditing: A Journal of Practice & Theory American Accounting Association*, Vol. 32, No. 3. August 2013, pp. 31–67 Available at: https://pdfs.semanticscholar.org/6a2c/ b8338898ad1ca1449aa68a88e680535978a5.pdf Accessed April 2017.

3 Velte, P., and Stiglbauer, M., 2012, 'Audit market concentration and its influence on audit quality', *International Business Research*, Vol. 5, October 2012, pp. 146–161. Available at: www.researchgate.net/publication/257923443_

Audit_Market_Concentration_and_Its_Influence_on_Audit_Quality Accessed April 2017.

4 Xie, F., 2016, 'Competition, auditor independence and audit quality', PhD thesis, University of Hawaii, December 2016. Available at: https://scholarspace.manoa.hawaii.edu/bitstream/10125/51624/1/2016-12-phd-xie.pdf Accessed January 2018.

5 Ibid. Xie has an excellent and current literature review.

6 *Financial Reporting Council News*, 2018, 'FRC response to Sir John Kingman's call for evidence'. Available at: ewww.frc.org.uk/news/june-2018/frc-response-to-sir-john-kingman's-call-for-evid Accessed June 2018.

7 In April 2018 the government launched an independent review of the FRC, the regulator for auditors, accountants and actuaries. The review will be led by Sir John Kingman, who has extensive private and public sector experience. He will be supported by an advisory board. The root and branch review, due for completion by the end of 2018, will assess the FRC's governance, impact and powers, to help ensure it is fit for the future.

8 Urwin, R., 2018, 'FRC: The watchdog that barked too late: After a string of corporate collapses, has the accounting regulator finally found its teeth?', *The Sunday Times*, 8 July 2018. Available at: www.thetimes.co.uk/article/frc-the-watchdog-that-barked-too-late-qln3xg7zh Accessed April 2018.

9 Ibid.

10 Kingman Review, 2018, 'Independent review of the financial reporting council', *Review Secretariat Which Is Hosted by the Department for Business, Energy, and Industrial Strategy*, 6 June. Available at: https://assets.publishing.service.gov.uk/government/uploads/system/uploads/attachment_data/file/717492/Independent_Review_of_the_FRC_-_Call_for_Evidence_-_FINAL.pdf Accessed July 2018.

11 Ibid.

12 Marriage, M., 2018, 'UK accountancy watchdog's competence faces government probe: Business secretary criticises operations of Financial Reporting Council', *Financial Times*, 21 March 2018. Available at: www.ft.com/content/985c8a04-2d29-11e8-a34a-7e7563b0b0f4 Accessed July 2018.

13 Fino, J., 2018, 'Greg Clark considering independent review of FRC', *Economia*, March 2018. Quotes taken from *Economia* and reproduced with kind permission of ICAEW. https://economia.icaew.com/. © ICAEW 2018. Available at: https://economia.icaew.com/en/news/march-2018/greg-clark-considering-independent-review-into-frc Accessed April 2018.

14 Members of the board of an entity producing annual and corporate reports – in general with or without accounting qualifications.

15 Chu, B., 2016, 'Theresa May's great crusade against big business fat-cats has lapsed into minor tinkering', *Independent*, 29 November 2016. Available at: www.gov.uk/government/news/independent-review-of-the-financial-reporting-council-frc-launches-call-for-evidence Accessed June 2018.

16 Jonathan Riley, head of quality and reputation at the accountancy firm Grant Thornton as reported in Urwin, 'FRC: The watchdog that barked too late: After a string of corporate collapses, has the accounting regulator finally found its teeth?'.

17 Ibid.

18 Masters, B., 2017, 'KPMG scandal highlights problem of auditing's revolving door: Five partners at accountancy firm failed to act on danger posed by secret tipster', *Financial Times*, 13 April 2017. Available at: www.ft.com/content/e891ae78-2023-11e7-a454-ab04428977f9 Accessed June 2017.

19 A student of Krish and John's at the University of Bristol.

20 Doherty, R., 2014, 'FRC drops PwC Berkeley investigation', *Economia*, 12 June 2014 Quotes taken from *Economia* and reproduced with kind permission of ICAEW. https://economia.icaew.com/. © ICAEW 2018. Available at: https://economia.icaew.com/news/june-2014/frc-drops-pwc-berkeley-investigation Accessed May 2015.

21 It was reported that PwC opened the bidding for firms interested in buying Carillion's rail division along with a number of the company's road maintenance and facilities management contracts. Simpson, J., 2018, 'PwC to sell Carillion's rail division', *Construction News*, 8 February 2018. Available at: www.construc tionnews.co.uk/companies/contractors/carillion/pwc-to-sell-carillions-rail-division/10027980.article Accessed April 2018.

22 Hosking, P., 2018, 'Regulator under pressure as Big Four battle plans for reform', *The Sunday Times*, 17 March 2018. Available at: www.thetimes.co.uk/article/reg ulator-under-pressure-as-big-four-battle-plans-for-reform-6q5m60l6w Accessed April 2018.

23 Ibid.

24 Urwin, R., 2018, 'FRC: The watchdog that barked too late: After a string of corporate collapses, has the accounting regulator finally found its teeth?', 8 July 2018. Available at: www.thetimes.co.uk/article/frc-the-watchdog-that-barked-too-late-qln3xg7zh

25 Izza, M., 2018, 'Breaking up the Big Four', *ICAEW Communities*, posted 16 March 2018. Quotes taken from Michael Izza and reproduced with kind permission of ICAEW. © ICAEW 2018. Available at: https://ion.icaew.com/moorgateplace/b/weblog/posts/breaking-up-the-big-four Accessed April 2018.

26 Leaders, 2018, 'Shape up, not break up: Reforming the Big Four', *The Economist*, May 2018. Available at: www.economist.com/leaders/2018/05/26/reforming-the-big-four Accessed May 2018.

27 Fino, J., 2018, 'FRC seeks to expand auditors' responsibilities', *Economia*, 4 April 2018. Quotes taken from *Economia* and reproduced with kind permission of ICAEW. https://economia.icaew.com/. © ICAEW 2018. Available at: https://economia.icaew.com/en/news/april-2018/frc-seeks-to-expand-auditors-responsibilities?utm_campaign=Members%20-%20ICAEW&utm_medium=email&utm_source=389722_economia_6April18&utm_content=frc&dm_i=47WY,8CPM,KDWTA,WNS4,1 Accessed April 2018.

28 These two references are typical of many: www.ipe.com/pensions/pensions/pensions-accounting/frc-under-fire-over-accountability-links-to-uk-audit-pro fession/10021436.article; www.taxresearch.org.uk/Blog/2017/10/17/how-many-audit-failures-will-it-take-for-the-frc-to-admit-that-the-failures-are-systemic/.

29 Bouvier, S., 2017, 'FRC under fire over accountability, links to UK audit profession', *IPE* (*Intelligence on European Pensions and Institutional Investment*), 31 October 2017. Available at: www.ipe.com/pensions/pensions/pensions-accounting/frc-under-fire-over-accountability-links-to-uk-audit-profession/10021436.article Accessed November 2017.

30 Ibid.

31 Smith, P., 2017, 'FTSE 100 alumni survey 2017: Big Four dominate boardrooms and regulator', *Accountancy Daily/Magazine*, 4 December 2017. Available at: www.accountancydaily.co/ftse-100-alumni-survey-2017-big-four-dominate-board rooms-and-regulator Accessed December 2017.

6 Audit disruption and new technology

Digital technologies that will affect reporting and auditing

Digital technology is developing at a pace. This chapter concentrates mainly on artificial intelligence (AI) because that is the sphere that we believe will impact on the audit market most significantly. AI has to the power to change the audit market in a disruptive way just as Uber, AirBnb, Netflix and Amazon have changed their sectors.

We have noted that so far reporting and auditing have failed to keep up with, or make any headway amongst the new developments we've reviewed. A number of standard accounting packages have kept pace with the best and latest technology, although the cost of switching can be prohibitive.

The technological developments which may affect accounting and reporting are many and varied.

- Devices vary from mainframes, mini and micro computers, work-stations and PCs, then laptops, tablets, smart phones, the ill-fated Google glasses, watches, and devices that are embedded in clothes. Input devices are increasingly mimicking humans (voice input), and are also being automated.
- The Internet of Things (IoT) is the network of physical devices, vehicles, home appliances and other items embedded with electronics, software, sensors, actuators and connectivity which enables these objects to connect and exchange data. Each item is uniquely identifiable through its embedded computing system but is able to interoperate within the existing internet infrastructure. We predict that the IoT will consist of about 50 billion objects by 2025 with a global market value of IoT of over £10 trillion.
- Multi-media (text, animation, graphics, photos, images and video) are now more or less standard. More is to come.

- Cables are being replaced by wireless technology. The 4G mobile network will metamorphose into 5G and 6G and onwards.
- Networking among computers and devices is standard as are databases – distributed and cloud based.
- Cloud computing is in its infancy but is already about to be replaced. Security and privacy apart, just about everything can be kept and processed in the cloud as wireless networks become exponentially faster with a rapidly increasing bandwidth.
- Fog and Edge computing extends the paradigm of cloud computing to the edge of the network, thereby facilitating information generation and analytics to occur at the source of the data. The term Fog computing metaphorically conveys the idea that the advantages of cloud computing could be brought closer to data source just as fog is cloud that is close to the ground.
- Accounting systems are more and more dominated by purchased application software. These include big software companies, financial packages specialists (Xero, QuickBooks, Sage and about 50 others), generalized systems such as Accodex, tax systems, and the Big Four's own systems. The range of software packages is likely to reduce through mergers, concentration and some suppliers dropping out of the market. (However, we think the number of offerings is likely to increase in Asia, for language/cultural reasons.)
- Internet, intranets, e-commerce are already well established but there is change of an order of magnitude yet to come.
- Businesses have yet to make much use of neural networks, Bayesian probability, artificial intelligence or intelligent knowledge-based systems. But the use of such systems will explode during the next decade.

Grey information and analytics

The World Wide Web that you can see and visit is only one five hundredth of the total web. Cloud computing and big data[1] all add to a rate of change. So, what is visible or can be found by search engines is a fraction of what is in the web. There will be over 50 billion devices connected to the internet by 2025 (with a world population of seven billion). Parts of Asia, and particularly China, will be well ahead of the West in this respect.

Big data, social media, messaging apps and grey data

Grey information includes big data, cloud computing, mobile apps, social media, games, private intranets, deep web, dark web and many more digital apps and web storage applications.[2] This includes both information that a company owns and third-party sites (for example, information collected by Facebook, Google and others on everyone, analytic sites, social network interactions/analysis sites and so on).

Big data is sometimes defined as extremely large data sets, including all grey data that may be analyzed computationally to reveal patterns, trends and associations, especially relating to human behaviour and interactions. The distinguishing feature is that in order to find meaningful patterns, much IT investment is necessary to manage and maintain that data.

In theory, social media are computer-mediated technologies that facilitate the creation and sharing of information, ideas, career interests and other forms of expression via virtual communities and networks. In practice, they have split down to Facebook type sites, Twitter type sites, messaging (WhatsApp, Messenger, etc.) and then specialist sites dealing with photos, music, dating or a host of other functions. Facebook is ahead in harvesting information on an individual level. Facebook's data harvesting and targeting is simply awe inspiring and it continues to gather more and more information – despite privacy concerns.

E-commerce

Electronic or e-commerce is a way of doing business over large electronic networks. E-commerce greatly facilitates transactions between companies and consumers (B2C), between one company and another (B2B), and between individual consumers (C2C) – via sites such as eBay. The exponential growth of e-commerce is unstoppable. Amazon UK has about 16% (but growing fast) of the market followed by Tesco (9%) and then eBay (8%).[3]

Digital footprint

Every time anyone comes on to a website, they leave a digital footprint, including their email address, actual address, telephone numbers and all the information available on that person held in Google, Bing, Facebook, Safari and other sites. This data is hugely valuable and the types of use and extents to which the big tech companies can use it is frightening. There is more customer data available than ever before. This data can also be used by auditors and therefore has implications for auditing.

Analytics

Analytics, or more correct, data analytics, is the discovery, interpretation and communication of meaningful patterns in data. It is most commonly applied to online information. In theory, this is especially valuable in areas rich with recorded information. Analytics relies on the simultaneous application of statistics, computer programming and operations research to quantify performance. In practice this is typified by Google Analytics which offers a (partly)[4] free enterprise analytics tools to measure website, app, digital and offline data to gain customer insights.

Of course, the most obvious information is about visitors to a site and their profiles. Then any interaction, conversion goal or transaction details on the site, and what visitors are also doing on other parts of the web too. The number of visitors, retention, conversion rates, time on site, new versus returning, loyalty of customer visits, income group, gender, location, device, operating system, screen size, reach, frequency are all important metrics and can be recorded by analytics and subsequently be analyzed and reported. Again this has implications for auditors and can used by auditors.

Possible impact of these technologies on auditing

Blockchain accounting

Forget the hype – a blockchain is a very simple concept: it is just a secure distributed ledger. The encryption process is ultra-secure as a number of people process the same transaction simultaneously and agree the result. Such people are called blockchain miners. See Appendix 1.06.1 for a further discussion. By and large the benefits of blockchains have been overstated.

Accounting ledgers merging

So taken as a given – we assume an advanced form of accounting using a new innovative multi-entry accounting spliced into a relational type database and using blockchains. Blockchains allow the possibility of having a single worldwide ledger containing all business and banking transactions[5] (at least in theory). That is probably too extreme, but certainly it would be possible to have a country-wide blockchain for accounting transactions. Or more likely several competing blockchains with an import and export facility. Or possibly an industry-specific, or regional blockchain for accounting transactions. It is also possible for the Big Four to run their own accounting blockchains for their client accounts and then hand over that portion of the blockchain to the rotating auditor.

At the moment all of the Big Four offer a range of blockchain applications and services. They are likely to grow, though there is resistance from the FTSE companies because they already have their hands full with other technological developments. It is commonly acknowledged that Deloitte was an early adopter of blockchain with its Rubix system launched in 2014. It also created a blockchain lab in Dublin, Ireland. But the other three firms have all now launched a variety of initiatives.

The more companies sign up to a single accounting blockchain the more efficient it is and the easier to verify transactions, report on them and to audit them. However, it would probably require government action to achieve such a result. (See Appendix 1.06.2 for a discussion of cryptocurrencies. This too has been over-hyped.)

Data mining

One area that is particularly interesting for auditors is data mining techniques (not to be confused with blockchain or Bitcoin mining). Data mining is the process of discovering patterns in large data sets involving methods at the intersection of statistics, database systems and big data. It is an essential process in auditing where intelligent methods are applied to extract data patterns. For auditors, data mining can provide verification and authentication data.

Auditing impacts and extensions

Auditing has to stretch to encompass all grey data and of course the Internet of Things. Text messages on smart phones and social media comments will be vital too for an overall knowledge of the group being audited. If the senior executives at Steinhoff (see Chapter 8 in *Financial Failures & Scandals: From Enron to Carillion* in this series) had had their phones and all communications monitored by the auditors, then either there would not have been a set of missing items in the balance sheet or the allegedly fraudulent transactions would not have happened. It may sound far-fetched, but something akin to a 'big brother' approach in business has to be considered especially if the auditor is in some way liable or faces much greater fines or consequences.

Artificial intelligence (AI)

This is the big development for auditing. Gilly Lord, head of audit strategy and transformation at PwC, agrees that AI is rapidly transforming the face of audit for the Big Four, allowing them to analyze huge data sets with mind-boggling speed and efficiency.[6]

We agree but even so, think that is a far too narrow view. The tech giants are going much further. The big battle with AI systems is whether there should be one giant generalized AI system capable of doing everything (or a series of them) or whether we have more specialized AI systems. Google/Deep Mind are in favour of one all-powerful generalized AI system. Elon Musk (Tesla, Space X among others) was an initial investor into Google's Deep Mind, but left Deep Mind – which is now 100% owned by Alphabet (Google's parent since 2014).

In December 2015, Musk announced the creation of OpenAI, a not-for-profit artificial intelligence research company. OpenAI aims to develop artificial general intelligence in a way that is safe and beneficial to humanity. By making AI available to everyone, OpenAI wants to:

> counteract large corporations who may gain too much power by owning super-intelligence systems devoted to profits, as well as governments which may use AI to gain power and even oppress their citizenry.[7]

Musk has stated he wants to counteract the concentration of power. In 2018 Musk left the OpenAI board to avoid 'potential future conflict' with his role as CEO of Tesla as Tesla increasingly becomes involved in AI. The type of AI in Tesla cars or Google's Waymo, or Uber's self-driving car systems (currently some of the most advanced autonomous intelligent driving systems), is an example of a narrow, specialized AI system.

Definitions

AI is not so much the application of human reasoning techniques by machines. We suggest that this is the wrong way to look at it. There are at least three basic core components that define the totality of artificial intelligence and expert decisions and the lesser intelligent knowledge-based systems. Traditionally such systems have been defined as knowledge bases, databases and database management systems, inference engines, user interfaces and knowledge-acquisition components. But that can be broken down into:

1) systems which implement decision rules based on some type of data input;
2) systems as above but that interact with some sort of dynamic database in order to make a decision. The decision rules may be modified over time by the new data;
3) machine learning systems. As above, but with the true capability of the decision rules learning from past mistakes or success. In this case, there has to be some feedback mechanism to report back on past decisions.

As we have seen AI systems can be broken down into a) narrower special-ized systems (such as driverless cars as above) or b) generalized AI systems. There is always an element of machine learning where a computer system is fed large amounts of data, which it then uses to learn how to carry out specific tasks. Narrower AI is what we see all around us in computers today: intelligent systems that have been taught or have learned how to carry out specific tasks without being explicitly programmed how to do so. Your fridge may be automatically filled without human interaction; products are bought, meals cooked before any human decision is made; entertainment is automatically served; holidays automatically booked.

Generalized AI systems are very different and mimic a type of adapt-able intellect found in humans, which is a flexible form of intelligence capable of learning how to carry out vastly different tasks. The difference is they are specialized in everything and there is nothing they cannot do.

Machine learning

Machine learning is the vital part of AI that often uses algorithms to enable computers to 'learn', i.e. to progressively improve performance on a specific task – without being explicitly programmed.

Key to the process of machine learning are neural networks. These are brain-inspired networks of interconnected layers of algorithms, called neurons, that feed data into each other, and which can be trained to carry out specific tasks by modifying the importance attributed to input data as it passes between the layers. During training of these neural networks, the weights attached to different inputs will continue to be varied until the output from the neural network is very close to what is desired, at which point the network will have 'learned' how to carry out a particular task.

A subset of machine learning is deep learning, where neural networks are expanded into sprawling networks with a huge number of layers that are trained using massive amounts of data. Remember that a neural net is a function of a bunch of weights. By adjusting the weights, you can make the function behave differently. The machine learning works by doing the same operation millions or billions of times until it gets closer to the ideal or winning situation. One can see how this works for self-driving cars – you let the system drive for months on end and the degree of intervention by a human driver will gradually tail off. It is more difficult to see how this would apply to auditing; nonetheless we believe it will – just that the mathematics of the algorithm is more like the human brain including a degree of fuzziness and intuition.

Advanced AI techniques use vast layers of neural networks with tech-niques such as backpropagation and reinforcement learning. The next technique is for AI systems to be self-programming – avoiding the need of any human intervention. Evolutionary computation is the process of using AI to help build AI. The use of evolutionary algorithms to optimize neural networks is called neuroevolution, and could have an important role to play in helping design efficient AI as the use of intelligent systems becomes more prevalent. Deep Mind uses many hundreds of layers of neural networks to facilitate fast learning. Google and Microsoft have moved to using specialized chips tailored to both running, and training, machine learning AI systems.

Some studies say that AI will evolve slowly[8] but we believe that whatever you may read about the speed of AI systems coming into the mainstream, you should think again. We believe the chances that AI will become commonplace by 2030 are great. Accounting, financial and auditing are prime suspects for their application. Think of the complexity of IFRS as it now, and then add an order of magnitude of more complexity. Think about the ever-expanding (currently 24 volumes or so) FCA handbook.

AI and the Big Four

Consider the common objective of the big accounting/auditing firms – to make a profit. All the Big Four have various AI systems and are developing more. Then think of AI systems becoming increasingly cheap through the use of Alphabet/Google and other open-source AI modules as part of their overall makeup, making AI systems more affordable. It is possible and perhaps likely that one of the tech giants or unicorns will develop an audit AI engine.

Of course, each of the Big Four will each say their AI system has a special characteristic and is better. KPMG has their advanced AI package called Ignite. Deloitte partnered with Kira systems. All the Big Four have or are using IBM's Watson AI package. PwC is experimenting with autonomous drones, and as its mantra goes, 'AI will become part of PwC's DNA'. Deloitte has raised the concept of robotics for audits. But whatever we say about the current use of AI by the Big Four will soon be out of date. Although, there is another albeit unlikely possibility: an AI audit system if sufficiently cheap could undermine the Big Four's scale advantages.

Gilly Lord has talked publicly about PwC's use of machine learning to audit journals. This is what two senior members of the Big Four have publicly said:

> We've not told it what to look out for, such as journals posted on a Saturday night or unusual amounts or unusual account combinations.

The more journals and the bigger population you feed it, the better it gets at identifying what is a real anomaly.

One of Lord's colleagues piloted the machine learning in parallel with the regular human investigation of the data analyzed on a recent audit. The results, she says, were fascinating.

The machine is identifying fewer anomalies for investigation – but it turned out that these were the real anomalies, the ones we needed to spend time on.[9]

Nick Frost, KPMG head of audit technology, said that some analytic tools are being applied to judgements that are based on predictions, such as asset impairment. These tools can review a client's forecasts for recovery of an asset and then apply predictive algorithms against those forecasts to come up with a probable value of the cash the asset will generate. What used to be a manual process is transformed into a multiple-scenario model that can be used to challenge the client's judgement. Frost says that these tools are incredibly powerful.

Now I can sit in front of an audit committee and say I am 90% sure that this asset is worth what you think it is. That's something I could not have done without the predictive algorithm.[10]

Technology and change in the audit process (practical considerations in the long run – 2025 onwards)

We will now consider AI systems for accounting and management information, operational systems. Let's assume that our subject area will use narrower specialized AI systems, i.e. even if they are generalized AI systems, they will be allocated a narrow, specialized task.

Accounting, in a multiple-entry system, will be performed by the firm's information system AI. It may also run all the management information systems and data collection necessary to take up an expanded reporting function, including much more non-financial information. If required, the AI system could produce the equivalent of an annual report every day using multiple accounting rules and multiple currencies. (Obviously, it will have access to all the accounting standards and have a view, or range of views, of what is true and fair.)

An operational AI will run the website, factories, organize supplies, make decisions if the factory is entirely automated, re-programme robots and run the customer systems. This operational AI provides information to the information system AI. Imagining an internal audit AI system which interacts with the information system AI is not a stretch of the imagination. The interactions between these sub-AI systems can occur seamlessly. The audit AI system can interrogate the information system AI system. The final addition is the reporting AI system which can create standard or tailored reports to anyone with sufficient privileges and permissions.

Then there would be the external auditor's AI system. Without even considering the job implications, there are three pitfalls. The tech giants claim that each can be overcome quite easily and quickly but they still need to be overcome.

1) At some point the system has to learn. During that learning phase mistakes will be made. The case studies demonstrate that failures do occur, there are no two which are exactly alike. For example, on revenue recognition, the AI would have to be able to predict the likelihood of, for example, customers not paying up for either a good reason or some trumped-up reason. Will the AI systems learn from its mistakes in revenue recognition? An audit AI system will be constantly learning as regulations change and the economic and commercial environment changes. Perhaps that AI system is better able to adapt. But during the learning phase, errors might occur.

2) AI systems need to explain how they reached a certain decision or conclusion, or in accounting terms, a certain value. At the moment AI systems are notorious for not being able to explain how the hundreds of layers of neural networks actually reached a decision. You might need a second AI to monitor the first AI in order to explain its decision-making process. Although a solution will eventually evolve, even Google's Deep Mind is not finding this process easy (but surmountable).

3) Then there is the problem that AI systems can communicate between themselves even if they are initially programmed not to. As AI systems can programme themselves, there is nothing to stop the audit AI system conspiring to do something with the company's information AI system. Maybe it could be just an agreement between the two AI systems to overlook something that subsequent events proved to be important. No one would know as the systems would specifically ensure that such communications and misstatements were covered

or within acceptable boundaries. Such communications may be for a very good reason – to protect the viability of the firm being audited, and the audited AI system would be in some way bought off to turn a blind eye. So conspiring for small creative accounting or even the equivalent of AI fraud would be a real possibility.

There are some other issues which need to be considered:

1) Edge cases are complicated and unusual situations that cannot be foreseen during training or machine learning. AI systems are pattern-recognition engines, trained on thousands of examples in the hope that the rules they infer will continue to apply in the wider world. But they apply those rules blindly, without a human-like understanding of what they are doing or an ability to improvise a solution on the spot. Designers of AI systems worry how their machines will perform in edge cases.[11]
2) It will be some time before AI systems can work in auditing. We are probably talking about sometime past 2025 and possibly past 2030. But the rate of progress, including that being researched, invested in and offered by the Big Four, and others, shows that a time frame of 2025 is possible for some of our predictions to have started to occur. The effects of such progress will manifest itself before the middle of the 2020s.

Such fundamental technological evolutions, like the Internet and mobile phones, quickly populate the world and then evolve very quickly into a rapidly expanding technology with new versions or disruptive start-ups being launched every year. With this pace of change, it is likely that some new entrants will take the standard routines of Deep Mind, OpenAI and others, and will be able to make our reporting, information processing and audit AI systems work effectively. It will not always be the big tech companies or the Big Four that will launch the new revolutionary ways and we think that there may be some new players.

We leave the last word to Hywel Ball, Head of assurance at EY who put this succinctly:

> New technology is already having a big impact on the audit pro-fession and the pace of change will only continue to accelerate. . . . Data analytics, artificial intelligence and robotic process automation are changing both what and how we audit. Enabling us to search, sift and sort through large quantities of data, from company reports to social media, these tools are helping auditors to identify potential areas of risk and to understand a company's performance at a more

granular level. They are also providing insights into areas that were once thought to be impossible to measure, such as culture. . . . The availability of new technology and explosion of big data are also raising important questions around how audit delivers value in the knowledge economy. We have never before had so much information available about organisations' performance, and yet many companies are struggling to tell a clear story to their investors and other stakeholders about the long-term value they are creating. Added to a general declining trust in business, and it is clear that the audit profession has some big challenges if it is to reflect the changing demands of society.[12, 13]

Notes

1 Big data is a broad term for data sets so large or complex that traditional data processing applications are inadequate. Challenges include analysis, capture, data curation, search, sharing, storage, transfer, visualization and information privacy. Most of this data is kept on web (private or public).

2 Not just the WWW.

3 'The top 500 ecommerce retailers in the UK' *Ecommerce News Europe*, 10 February 2017. Available at: https://ecommercenews.eu/top-500-ecommerce-retailers-uk/ Accessed July 2017.

4 You have to pay for certain parts and certain more detailed data.

5 See this FRC publication for an excellent description of blockchains. We just disagree with their conclusion as to the speed and usage. Financial Reporting Council Lab, 2018, 'Blockchain and the future of corporate reporting: How does it measure up?', *Financial Reporting Lab, Financial Reporting Council*, June 2018. Available at: www.frc.org.uk/news/june-2018/publication-of-the-financial-reporting-lab's-repor Accessed June 2018.

6 Munro, R., 2018, 'Artificial intelligence and machine learning in accountancy – Part 1', *Accountancy Daily/Magazine*, 5 June 2018. Available at: www.accountancydaily.co/artificial-intelligence-and-machine-learning-accountancy-part-1 Accessed June 2018.

7 Clifford, C., 2018, 'Elon Musk: "Mark my words – A.I. is far more dangerous than nukes"', *CNBC Make It*, 13 March 2018. Available at: www.cnbc.com/2018/03/13/elon-musk-at-sxsw-a-i-is-more-dangerous-than-nuclear-weapons.html Accessed April 2018.

8 Stanford University, 2017, '100 year study on AI kicks off its next report cycle', *One Hundred Year Study on Artificial Intelligence (AI100)*. Available at: https://ai100.stanford.edu/ Accessed April 2018.

9 Biebuyck, C., 2017, 'Audit automation', *Economia*, 7 September 2017. Quotes taken from *Economia* and reproduced with kind permission of ICAEW. https://economia.icaew.com/. © ICAEW 2017. Available at: https://economia.icaew.com/en/features/september-2017/audit-automation Accessed November 2017.

10 Ibid.

11 See for example: Leaders, 2018, 'The Kamprad test: IKEA furniture and the limits of AI', *The Economist,* 21 April 2018. Available at: www.economist.com/news/

leaders/21740735-humans-have-had-good-run-most-recent-breakthrough-robotics-it-clear Accessed May 2018.

12 Wilcox, R., 2018, '2018: What's in store for accountants in the year ahead?', *Accountancy Daily/Magazine*, 2 January 2018. Available at: www.accountancydaily.co/2018-whats-store-accountants-year-ahead Accessed January 2018.

13 The FRC published an excellent paper on AI in January 2019. Artificial intelligence and corporate reporting. Available at: https://www.frc.org.uk/getattachment/e213b335-927b-4750-90db-64139aee44f2/AI-and-Corporate-Reporting-Jan.pdf Accessed January 2019.

7 Disruptive audit structures

Splitting up the Big Four

Introduction

This chapter is concerned with the possible options for splitting up the Big Four into smaller units. In the next chapter we evaluate these alternatives. Unless the Big Four voluntarily agree to split themselves up (and there is no sign in the short term that they will) any reorganization or restructuring of the audit market and the Big Four will take time. That said, as the FT reported,[1] Greg Clark, the Business Minister, said the government has called for a 'sweeping' review of Britain's auditing industry. This raises concerns that the government would back major reforms to the Big Four. The minister has asked the CMA to examine competition in the audit industry dominated by the Big Four.

See Appendix 1.07.1 for a summary of the criticisms of the Big Four and audit market up to this point and Appendix 1.07.2 for a discussion on the international network issues which affect the Big Four. See http://www.fin-rep.org/which-book/disruption-to-the-audit-market/ for our response to the CMA report and other updates.

Survival of the Big Four (with no split)

Before discussing the possible split scenarios, there may be one other factor which might make such discussion irrelevant. That is if the Big Four fail or become the Big Three. The usual assumption is that viability of the Big Four may not be threatened in the UK because of the Caparo precedent which provides a measure of protection against court cases against the external auditors,[2] but in the US there is no such limit. Court cases are common. In 2013, Deloitte settled (for an undisclosed sum) a life-threatening $7.5 billion claim by the trustee of the criminally driven bankruptcy of mortgage lender Taylor Bean & Whitaker.[3] But that danger is always present. Jim Petersen raised this possibility in his book[4] and in various articles:[5]

> That news – along with the size of the number, when it eventually surfaces – should trouble all those not evading the reality that "Black Swan" litigation could trigger the catastrophically viral collapse of the Big Four – a possibility beyond denial given the death spiral of Arthur Andersen in 2002. The only sure alternative, I have believed, is the resolution, on a pre-collapse basis, of the seemingly intractable impediments to a sustainable audit function for the future – including the Big Four's persistent performance quality challenges, litigation liability, financial fragility, un-insurability, and independence-based constraints on their scope of services.

However, the demise of the US Big Four partnerships would not necessarily affect the UK and European partnerships. So, on balance, we believe the Big Four are probably secure in the UK, even if their American counterparts may not be. But of course that may change with legislation or changes to the Companies Act that may be made post-Carillion. So auditors may find that they are more liable to third-party actions with some future change. How this will affect them is discussed in the next chapter.

We had thought that the Big Four were not vulnerable in the UK, but that has changed. It is rumoured that the PRA, the Bank of England's watchdog, which supervises the UK's largest banks and insurers, has raised questions about the risks to KPMG's viability. These risks include UK issues, the biggest of which was Carillion and a major loss of clients in South Africa, following allegations of scandals involving its work for the controversial Gupta family in South Africa – losing at least 20 clients. KPMG might possibly be facing new restrictions in South Africa. There are also problems in the US where the US watchdogs charged three former KPMG partners with leaking confidential information in a bid to improve inspection results in January 2018.[6]

So Petersen's claim that one of the Big Four could fail may not be so far removed. Oliver Shah, the legendary business editor of the *Sunday Times* posits a pet theory about KPMG's troubles.[7] However, the situation is, we believe, more complicated and endemic to the Big Four – it is the way they currently think. KPMG, we believe, will survive and prosper but the firm has to be careful. If it did fail then all bets are off. In this event, not only, do we think, would the Big Four consulting divisions be hived off, but also the audit divisions would be broken up in some way.

Certainly, we would not be left with the Big Three but with a Big Six or some such number for the big auditing firms. This would occur for the UK, probably Europe and Africa, but perhaps also spill over into the US/ North America. The international networks would become realigned, as they have done in Asia and elsewhere (and that it is not such a big event as is often claimed).

Peterson also argues that the Big Four might view their consulting divisions as more important than the audit divisions and therefore close the audit divisions. The outgoing partners and staff of the audit division would then create an audit-only division. He concludes:

> The eventual day of final reckoning for private audit would not be upon the withdrawal of the Big Four into the prosperity of consulting, but when one of their offspring should suffer the fate that only recently threatened Deloitte.[8]

But surely the Big Four want to keep an audit capacity for the sake of credibility? Peterson thinks not.

> [T]hat point is readily answered by experience: Accenture not only did not need an on-going relationship with its erstwhile accounting bedmate [Arthur Andersen which collapsed in 2002] – it could scarcely wait for the ink to dry on the divorce decree before scrubbing itself of prior history and maximising the distance between the two.[9]

A lively image. But when we questioned the Big Four in our series of interviews, it was clear that they all saw audit at the heart of the Big Four's DNA. Without audit they would become entirely different entities with different corporate cultures. An example to explain this is the fact that PwC is still trusted to oversee the Oscars film awards despite the mistakes made during the 2017 ceremony. It is the prestige that is conjured up by any one of the Big Four because of their auditing work – a public service (*a la* Oscars judicators and performed by PwC), over and above pure financial concerns.

Like Peterson, Gow and Kells are also critical of the Big Four, although not entirely rationally in our view. They argue that:

> The history of the 'Big Four' firms is one of triumphs and disasters, of pioneers and scoundrels. Today, the firms have an uncertain future – thanks to their push into China; their vulnerability to digital

disruption and competition; and the hazards of providing traditional tax and audit services in a new era of transparency.[10]

We do not share this view, though the possibility of standardized AI systems being a threat cannot be underestimated. We think each of the Big Four will wrap such systems with their own brand of novelty and distinctiveness.

> Both advisory and audit services are being disrupted, commoditised, digitised and offshored. The Big Four need to invest big to meet the disruption, but their franchise structure and partnership model are barriers to large-scale investment in the necessary innovations.[11]

There are signs of investment and innovation, but we agree:

> The leverage model[12] and the partner track depend on growth, but, given all these pressures, the current rate of Big Four growth is unsustainable. In the face of technological disruption, the firms are suffering an exodus of ideas and talent. They imagine they can control digital technologies and 'disrupt themselves'. They cannot.[13]

Growth is sustainable, we think, and may even increase if the current difficulties can be overcome. But the partnership structure and the pyramid personnel structure where the bottom layers are forced to work long hours with small salaries may not be sustainable. Not least because of competition from the tech giants and the start-ups, who pay larger salaries from the start with lots of benefits and a much nicer working environment. This is not concerned with splitting up as such but an evolution to a different type of Big Four firm with a narrower pyramid structure. We think this is bound to evolve. The current 'leverage' model (of personnel) is not sustainable. And in the future may not be considered even desirable. So the shape and *modus operandi* of the firms will, we believe, radically change. This has some implications for size, structure, ethics and culture. But we think we are talking about decades so this will not satisfy those who want change in the short or medium term.

Peterson[14] claims that a study investigating the viability of the Big Four shows that a critical number of partners would defect if faced with a financial commitment of an individual profit reduction of 15% to 20% extending over three to four years. We can't confirm that report. However, fines of £100m or so could be levied on any of the Big Four without damaging the entities themselves. But if this was done continually that might lead to a different conclusion. However, in relation to the individual named partner, the threat of a substantial fine and possible ban from the profession would in our view be a significant deterrent and that peer pressure also carries through to all senior staff on that audit. So we cannot see Peterson's claim ever coming to pass.

A warning though: the possibility of one of the Big Four failing in some way, though remote, remains a small finite risk. If that happens the Big Three would provide too little choice. Even in the UK, they are now too big to fail. The other three, with or without government support, would have to step in.

The options for splitting and the attendant difficulties

The favoured options for addressing the dominance of the Big Four are presently as outlined by the SC (page 85).[15] "We recommend that the Government refers the statutory audit market to the Competition and Markets Authority. The terms of reference of that review should explicitly include consideration of both":[16]

*   Breaking up the Big Four into more audit firms (say into eight units);
*   Detaching audit arms from those providing other professional and consulting services.

As we shall see, neither may be practicable. The Big Four are part of a huge international network.

On the demise of Arthur Andersen, the network went in a number of different ways depending on geography with Deloitte picking up the main share. When Deloitte and Touche Ross merged in 1989 the network split in at least two ways with the UK Deloitte not wanting to join Touche unlike the rest of the network. Instead, they joined Coopers & Lybrand (which then joined PwC). So historically, each region has had its own peculiarities.

The makeup of the network is secure in its present form. But if anything disturbs it, then the partners in each country's partnership will have their own say as to how to proceed. There is no necessary uniform outcome. Any break-up in the UK will have ramifications elsewhere. So the ripples from any UK reorganization may have far reaching international affects, many of which are unpredictable.

CMA and the ICAEW intervene: Big Four win?

The FRC review by the Kingman has ruled out issues of competition that sit with the CMA, particularly competition in the audit market.[17] So the FRC has handed responsibility for any structural change over to the CMA, although there may be some interaction between the CMA and the Kingman/FRC – especially in connection with audit quality. The Big Four may very well have persuaded the CMA that any break-up is unworkable. Of course, in the event of one more big corporate failure, all bets are off. At best, all we can say is the jury is out.

As the competition watchdog, the CMA has challenged the Big Six (Big Four plus BDO and GT) to find ways to improve choice in the auditing market. The motivation for this is that it could save the break-up of the Big Four. The *Times* reported that the chief executive of the CMA issued the challenge in meetings with the biggest accountants.[18] This was before the Greg Clark decision to refer the audit market to the CMA officially.

And

> Executives at PWC, KPMG, Deloitte and EY have seized on the opportunity to prevent the biggest shake-up in their firms' history. They held a secret dinner in the City to discuss possible solutions last month. Board members from BDO and Grant Thornton, the fifth and sixth biggest audit firms, and the ICAEW also attended the meeting. A competition lawyer was present to guard against unintentional collusion.[19]

The CMA responded that it was working closely with the FRC.[20]

> Speaking for the Big Four, Hywel Ball, EY's UK head of audit, said, "The CMA has challenged the profession to suggest some solutions to increase choice in the market. We are working with the ICAEW and the rest of the profession to respond to that challenge."[21]

So for the time being, the Big four may have persuaded both the CMA and the FRC that the size of their network and other issues make the scenario whereby the Big Four are broken up impossible. The CMA advocated additional scrutiny of audit committees (we disagree) and dual audits and other actions to help bolster the mid-tier/challenger firms (we disagree and would take decades). See http://www.fin-rep.org/which-book/disruption-to-the-audit-market/

Split: competition, independence and audit quality

In this section, we develop our last axiom concerning independence and its impact on audit quality. One of the major criticisms at the beginning of this chapter was the Big Four's lack of independence and lack of competition. So in examining the split hypothesis the question has to be asked: does increased competition (as measured by the number of firms competing) lead to higher quality audits? We know from our axiom 3 (developed in Chapter 5) that competition as measured by the number of firms has a positive impact on audit quality (in general). So a split would lead to greater competition and higher audit quality. So that leaves us to consider the impact of independence of audit quality.

There are a number of views. The measurement of audit quality is not precise and means different things to different people. The FRC has an exact and carefully designed measure but it is not the only measure. Jan Bouwens, Professor of Accounting at the Judge Business School, University of Cambridge, UK and the Managing Director of the Foundation for Auditing Research, said:

> a considerable amount of research over the past 40 years on this subject simply does not support these concerns. Among dozens of studies in leading journals, three auditing practices have been looked at in particular depth: first, the extent to which the accountant allows the company to manipulate results to show better financial conditions than underlying numbers warrant; second, the willingness of the accountant to issue a qualified going-concern opinion; and third, the extent to which the accountant holds on to the "conservatism principle" (recognising profit only if it is certain, while recognising uncertain losses). . . . However, research by leading academics over the past four decades hasn't found actual evidence of shortcomings that would lend support for sweeping policy changes in this regard. In fact, it is found that, with the provision of advisory services, audit firms extend their knowledge base.[22]

These are strong words. The question is, are his assumptions correct? How many articles? Are they still relevant in current times? We found some of the most recent and highly referred articles do not support Professor Bouwens's theses. One experienced accountant commented:

> Bouwens states that conservatism is no longer an overriding principle. I wonder how much that is behind some of the more aggressive accounting practices that have been behind scandals in the post IFRS era.

A 2014 ICAEW study[23] on audit quality and independence came to a different conclusion:

> Raised client concerns about perceptions of impairment to auditor independence from the provision of NAS [non-audit services] are supported both directly and indirectly by the review of the impact of

behavioural and cognitive factors on auditor judgement and auditor independence, and effects of such factors on the ability of auditors to conduct audit with the required degree of scepticism.

John believes that conflict of interest has always affected the quality of an audit and he is in complete disagreement with Professor Bouwens. He believes fundamentally and absolutely that the accountancy profession has been corrupted by the pursuit of profit from activities other than auditing (such as tax advice and consultancy) and that, to remedy the situation, the audit firm (that is, the entity that carries out audits) should be forbidden from undertaking any activity other than auditing.

Another recent article 'Does Big 4 Consulting Impair Audit Quality?'[24] appears to come to a slightly more positive conclusion. However, on reading the full paper, we are not entirely convinced. They say:

> Overall, our results suggest that a higher proportion of consulting revenue to total revenue at the accounting firm level is not associated with impaired audit quality; in fact, some results indicate that a higher proportion of consulting revenue is associated with improved audit quality. However, results of earnings response coefficient tests suggest that investors perceive a deterioration in audit quality when a higher proportion of accounting firm revenue is generated from consulting services.

Xie (2016)[25] found that audit market competition affects audit quality indirectly through enhanced auditor independence – the greater the independence the greater the audit quality (US data).

So, perception becomes important. Our final article, Kowaleski (2018) entitled 'The Impact of Consulting Services on Audit Quality: An Experimental Approach'[26] concludes

> We do not find differences in audit quality by condition in our planned analysis, however we find greater variation in audit quality in the conditions where auditors provide consulting services compared to the baseline. In unplanned analyses, our results suggest providing consulting services increases auditor cooperation with managers, increasing audit quality when managers prefer high audit quality and decreasing audit quality when managers prefer low audit quality.

The CMA offer some articles disproving this. Again we have provided a strong criticism of their conclusions. See http://www.fin-rep.org/wp-content/uploads/book2/5-Our-response-to-the-CMA-update-paper.pdf The fascinating aspect of this study is that the higher the consulting fee it seems the closer degree of cooperation. Reading between the lines, that cooperation means that management has a greater say over the type and style of the audit, or so it seems. Consultancy earnings makes the audit more compliant to management's wishes, exactly the reverse of Professor Bouwens's claims. His rigid rejection of any relationship between consulting and audit are not confirmed by more recent academic studies, our own evidence and by the ICAEW's study.

We think that the most recent literature seems to demonstrate a closer relationship between audit quality and independence – though this is a difficult variable to measure. That coupled with our own evidence indicates audit quality is positively correlated with greater independence. Krish and Rod think that the relationship, as far as there is one, is more subtle and not quite as direct as that claimed above – other causal factors are involved. We do not believe that simply splitting off the consulting divisions would improve audit quality. Other measures would be necessary if this were to happen. But we support and defend this final axiom:

Quality axiom 4: greater independence leads to higher audit quality.

Split: separation of consultancy

Krish and Rod can see the logic of separating consultancy services from audit but do not share this view. We think that the impact of ARD changed the process. The blacklist and the 70% non-audit fees cap mean that the consulting and audit divisions are already more separated and do not go after the same business at the same client – at least not at the same time. It should be noted however this does not currently apply to the same extent to SMEs and private companies. Separation of the PIEs and the major firms has occurred because of ARD. Rod defines this in terms of choosing between audit or consultancy – and that this is a sharp division within each of the Big Four which he believes is far more rigorously followed than the looser 70% cap restriction. There is always a tendency for audit work to expand to cover what may be defined strictly as non-statutory audit work.

The CMA has essentially dismissed any such split. Kingman, in a separate letter, supports such a split. We strongly criticize the CMA report.

Regardless of what the Kingman Review recommends, we think it is not going to make any difference. The actions of the CMA and its predecessors had little effect: what they did (together with the EU regulations) was to help increase concentration and reduce competition. Which of course is the exact opposite of the desired result.

In our interviews, it was clear that even before the audit reforms had been implemented, most of the Big Four senior partners saw this increase in concentration as a distinct possibility. But none of the Big Four did anything about it. This observation, together with many other interviews on the same topic, persuaded us that the Big Four knew that concentration would increase and competition would reduce. Perhaps they unwittingly welcomed it. The question now is can this be undone in some way?

Split: creating more choice and independence in the audit market

Instead of spitting up the Big Four, another way may be to build up the mid-tier so that they are of a similar size to the Big Four. This was much favoured by the CMA. They called these mid-tier challenger firms.

Developing and bolstering the mid-tier firms (called Challenger firms by the CMA)

It is surprising that the Big Four just sailed into this situation without appreciating the possible problems they were making for themselves. After all, the lack of competition in the field is a feature which attracts people's attention. There may be an argument to build up the competition. We now examine some possibilities with or without government intervention:

1) Grow BDO and GT to create the Big Six

The Big Four pay into a fund which provides a discount to the entity being audited if they go to the BDO or GT for the first 20 FTSE 100 companies and then the first 75 FTSE 250 or something similar. Even that may not be sufficient – you might have to have a secondary supervisory audit by one of the Big Four (without fees) in the first year of audit. To address international reach unavailable via BDO or GT (though they are significant internationally) then top-up services could be provided by one of the Big Four to provide an equivalence in term of geographical reach or industry coverage. This action was chosen by the CMA without due regard to the timing and consequences.

2) Merge a collection of mid-tier firms to make them larger and closer to the Big Four

In the past the mid-tier firms have had many mergers. One way to promote more competition in the industry would be more mergers among some of the mid-sized players in the audit market. They have a track record:

> To a varying degree, most of these have shown an appetite for such deals in the recent past. BDO and PKF joined forces in April 2013 and, in October that year, Baker Tilly and RSM Tenon announced that they

were merging. Moore Stephens, which for many years was renowned in the industry for not pursuing growth for the sake of it, merged with Chantrey Vellacott in May 2015 and followed this with last year's tie-up with the actuarial consulting firm James, Brennan & Associates.[27]

Mergers have continued apace since publication. See www.fin-rep.org

Elsewhere in the world, for example South Africa, such mergers are taking place. There are three problems:

a) It would require a combination of many of the mid-tier firms, to get anything approximating the Big Five. King[28] suggests for any meaningful rival to the Big Four to emerge from a merger, at least one of GT and BDO or RSM would need to be included and a combination of the next six largest UK audit firms to get to something even capable of turning the Big Four into a Big Five.

b) GT, BDO and some of the smaller mid-tier firms, such as Mzaar's (strong in Germany) have their own growth plans and culturally would be opposed to such mergers.

c) The attitude of clients and suspicion about pricing in the event of mergers. King[29] points to a negative experience in between 1985 and 2002 when some smaller clients and smaller listed companies often ended up having to pay more.

Nevertheless some sort of mergers especially if sweetened by the government may be a possibility.

3) Client cap by the Big Four or leave certain companies to the non-Big Four

The Big Four may be willing to consider placing limits on the number of listed audit clients the Big Four can have as a way of staving off a second formal competition complaint and possible break-up.[30] This could be achieved by segments of the FTSE 350.

Segment the FTSE 350 and/or the AIM 100 and allocate a section which, when they rotate, has to include mid-tier firms but none of the Big Four. A variation of this is for the Big Four to decide not to tender for certain classes of companies on the FTSE and AIM markets, forcing companies to go mid-tier. Those mid-tier companies could use the resources of one of the Big Four if necessary.

Another way is to have some sort of voluntary cap on markets share of the PIE audit market. King for example advocates:

a limit on the number of the top 350 UK companies that each firm can audit and phased in over the next five to ten years, looks one possible outcome. Another, which has been met with irritation from non-Big Four players, could see the quartet offer to lend technology or staff to smaller rivals.[31]

The CMA rejected this remedy.

Our views on building up the mid-tier firms

Rod is not impressed with any of the above. Nevertheless, we wanted to come up with some suggestions. With suitable constraints, Krish believes this might be workable. But size equates with quality – these mid-tier firms would have to grow substantially to be accepted. And yet increased competition may equal higher audit quality. So, this scenario goes, build up the mid-tier firms so that they have the size and provide more firms in the top league. Realistically this would take a decade or two as the Big Four are also growing apace.

Splitting: size does matter

Goldman Sachs, a leading global investment bank, has been reported as having held discussions with GT, the fifth largest audit firm and the largest mid-tier firm. This is in connection with a review of its audit relationship which is expected to rotate in the UK in 2022. The Bank of England and its associated regulator, the PRA, have both, more or less, objected to GT being the auditor. The *Times* reported:

> The Bank of England is examining whether an American investment bank may appoint an accountancy firm outside the Big Four as its British auditor over concerns that its chosen company lacks the resources of its elite rivals. . . . The PRA requires that an auditor of a British bank has the "required skill, resources and experience to perform its function under the regulatory system", according to its rule book. It has subjected new entrants to banking audits to scrutiny in the past, including questioning EY, one of the Big Four, about its resources and skills when it was appointed to audit Royal Bank of Scotland in 2014, which was then its biggest financial services client.[32]

Splitting the audit division and the consulting division into separate firms

Although the current battle to break up the Big For may be lost for now, we can further consider the independence aspect. A break-up of Britain's Big Four could address a crisis of confidence facing the sector after a series of scandals. The Big Four could be made to spin off their UK audit arms into separate businesses. The aim would be to increase competition and eliminate conflicts of interest arising from the dominance of the four firms.[33]

The question here is whether the 70% cap of non-audit to audit fees would still exist. If not then concentration might increase further. At Arthur Andersen and Andersen Consulting (which later became Accenture), projects arising from auditing work would be passed to the consulting company.

There is one set of circumstances which might lead to greater competition and more choice. Split the audit and consultancy divisions and give them completely independent status and a separate name. This could increase competition just as currently, if PwC provides consultancy services to a company, they cannot bid for the audit (unless relinquishing the [more profitable] consultancy work). However, if PwC Audit and Consultancy are totally separate firms (and without any shared branding), then we assume that the audit firm could bid, which would increase the number of times that an audit firm could tender for an account. Meanwhile, the consulting firm could pick up all the blacklist and consulting work they wanted without running into the non-audit cap fees of 70%.

Modelling the degree of freedom

To test the degree of freedom of choice we built a model to run experiments. Our simulation model analysis assumed the consulting and the audit divisions were completely separate and independent in the Big Four (with separated and clearly defined and different brand names). Choice increases – and can increase quite drastically. Given our best guess as to the starting position and current distribution of work, the audit choice increased by at least 50% and possibly by much more than 100% – a not insignificant gain. So if you had a choice of two, this would increase to three (50% increase). If you had a choice of one previously this would increase to three (a 200% increase). The exact calculation has to be probabilistic and depends on the starting point and the distribution and number of contracts and how they are currently spread among the Big Four (both audit and non-audit).

We experimented with a range of probabilities and starting points. In summary, our best estimate was that the degree of freedom of choice would increase by a factor of around 100% increase in choice over currently. This result surprised us and leads us to a more favourable perception of the split into audit-only and consultancy possibility. (See the volume on *Disruption in Auditing* for more information on the degree of freedom of choice.)[34]

Splitting: variations of break-ups

As we said before, the current battle to break up the Big For may be lost for now but we want to consider all the possibilities:

1) Split audit and consultancy (as above) and as suggested by the FRC: split the audit and consultancy division, separate the management, ensure there are no residual links between the two and rename the consultancy divisions. Make them completely independent. That alone would provide at least 50% and perhaps more than 100% more choice.

2) Split the Big Four into the Big Eight audit and consultancy firms. The brandname problems would be more intractable where two audit firms have been spun out of each of the Big Four.

3) Split audit creating eight audit firms, and the original four consulting firms. If each of the Big Four was to divide their audit divisions into two and was a separate and independent concern with different management structures, then this would double the number of audit firms, though they would not all have access to resources and technology. That would be split between the two new auditing entities or placed in a third service division.

Just a further word on splitting the Big Four into the Big Eight audit firms. You could go with the model of PSA's Peugeot-Citroen or the Hyundai-Kia branding model with two parallel but equal divisions. Or the VW model of tiers – luxury service with staff continuously on site, mid-level service and basic more functional level of service. Barriers would exist between each of the divisions which would compete. But this has potentially difficult international network problems as identified earlier.

Summary

We have now developed a number of options for splitting that we will evaluate in the next chapter. We have also developed our audit quality and independence axiom which are important in evaluating the options. In any split option, we do not want to make Carillion-type events more frequent; we want higher quality audits with the ability to prevent Carillion-type verdicts slipping through.

As we cautioned earlier, it may be that the Big Four have persuaded the CMA and the FRC that the network and other issues render the break-up scenario impossible or unworkable in the short run. However, as we explore in the next three chapters, there are other events and factors which may override this in the short run.

Notes

1 Parker, G., and Ford, J., 2018, 'Minister calls for probe into audit's Big Four', *Financial Times*, 29 September 2018. Available at: www.ft.com/content/73a7bb34–c338-11e8-8d55-54197280d3f7 Accessed September 2018.

2 Though this not unambiguous. There are counter-cases which re-establish some third-party liability.

3 In October 2013 Deloitte settled its US potentially damaging exposure to $7.5 billion in the Florida case brought by the bankruptcy trustee of Taylor Bean & Whitaker, the mortgage lender that collapsed in 2009 under several fraud charges. This led to prison sentences for its principals. This then led to PwC's US settling possible claims of $5.5 billion, brought by the same bankruptcy trustee Taylor Bean & Whitaker, relating to PwC's audits of the failed Colonial Bank. Both those settlement amounts were confidential and remain undisclosed today. That said the litigation outcomes at their worst could have come close to the break-up threshold of either firm, or had a significant impact on their finances. See this article from *Economia*, October 2013, for further information. Irvine, J., 2013, 'Deloitte settles over Taylor Bean', *Economia*, 4 October 2013. Quotes taken from *Economia* and reproduced with kind permission of ICAEW. https://eco nomia.icaew.com/. © ICAEW 2018. Available at: https://economia.icaew.com/news/october-2013/deloitte-settles-over-taylor-bean Accessed June 2016.

4 Peterson, J., 2017, *Count Down: The Past, Present and Uncertain Future of the Big Four Accounting Firm,* Emerald Publishing Limited, 2nd edition, July 2017. Available at: www.amazon.co.uk/Count-Down-Uncertain-Accounting-Development/dp/178560581X

5 Peterson, J., 2013, 'The Big Four's survival: Does consulting create an exit strategy?' *Re-Balance*, October 2013. Available at: www.jamesrpeterson.com/home/2013/10/the-big-fours-survival-does-consulting-create-an-exit-strategy.html Accessed April 2018.

6 For example see: Marriage, M., and Jenkins, P., 2018, 'Bank of England probed risks to KPMG's viability after string of scandals', *Financial Times*, 19 July 2018. Available at: www.ft.com/content/0fb845e0-8b5b-11e8-b18d-0181731a0340 Accessed July 2018. And Marriage, M., Bingham, C., and Arnold, M., 2018, 'Concerns raised about "too big to fail" KPMG', *Financial Times*, 19 July 2018. Available at: www.ft.com/content/f660b6a2-8b75-11e8-bf9e-8771d5404543 Accessed July 2018. And Marriage, M., 2018, 'KPMG loses 20 audit clients in South Africa since 2017', *Financial Times*, 3 August 2018. Available at: www.ft.com/content/bcaeba6a-9667-11e8-b747-fb1e803ee64e Accessed August 2018.

7 Shah, O., 2018, 'Oliver Shah: The music's over for accounting giants', *The Sunday Times*, 26 August 2018. Available at: www.thetimes.co.uk/article/oliver-shah-the-musics-over-for-accounting-giants-ldqzljzbh Accessed August 2018. Shah claims that former insiders trace KPMG's woes to an internal restructuring in 2015. Previously auditors had answered to the head of auditing, tax staff to the head of tax and so on (quite normal for the Big Four). Under the new changed

system, the divisions were organized around business sectors such as consumer and financial services.

8 Peterson, 'The Big Four's survival: Does consulting create an exit strategy?'.

9 Ibid.

10 Gow, I. D., and Kells, S., *The Big Four: The Curious Past and Perilous Future of the Global Accounting Monopoly*, La Trobe University Press, Carlton, Australia, 2018, p. 210. Available at: www.amazon.co.uk/dp/B077YCTV92/ref=dp-kindle-redirect?_ encoding=UTF8&btkr=1

11 Ibid.

12 See Chapter 3 for an explanation of this leverage term dealing with a flat pyramid model of personnel structure.

13 Ibid., p. 83.

14 Peterson, 'The Big Four's survival: Does consulting create an exit strategy?'; www.amazon.co.uk/Count-Down-Uncertain-Accounting-Development/dp/ 178560581

15 Ibid.

16 Ibid.

17 Kingman Review, 2018, 'Independent review of the financial reporting council', *Review Secretariat Which Is Hosted by the Department for Business, Energy, and Industrial Strategy,* 6 June. Available at: https://assets.publishing.service.gov. uk/government/uploads/system/uploads/attachment_data/file/717492/Inde pendent_Review_of_the_FRC_-_Call_for_Evidence_-_FINAL.pdf Accessed July 2018.

18 Kinder, T., 2018, 'Big Four are told to loosen grip on audits: Accountants hold secret talks to avoid break-up', *The Times*, 9 July 2018. Available at: www.thetimes. co.uk/article/big-four-are-told-to-loosen-grip-on-audits-tw9cc58d8 Accessed July 2018.

19 Ibid.

20 Fino, J., 2018, 'CMA challenges big audit firms to address competitiveness: the six biggest accountancy firms have met with ICAEW to discuss ways to improve competitiveness and prevent being broken up', *Economia*, 9 July 2018. Quotes taken from *Economia* and reproduced with kind permission of ICAEW. https:// economia.icaew.com/. © ICAEW 2018. Available at: https://economia.icaew. com/en/news/july-2018/cma-challenges-big-audit-firms-to-address-competi tiveness Accessed July 2018.

21 Ibid.

22 Bouwens, J., 2018, 'Evidence does not support "conflict of interest" worries', Letter, *Financial Times*, 20 March 2018. Available at: www.ft.com/content/78116a6a- 2b78-11e8-a34a-7e7563b0b0f4 Accessed May 2018.

23 Gwilliam, D., and Teng, C., M., 2014, 'How does joint provision of audit and non-audit services affect audit quality and independence?', ICAEW Charitable Trusts, 2014. Quotes taken from ICAEW and reproduced with kind permission of ICAEW. © ICAEW 2014. Available at: www.icaew.com/en/products/ audit-and-assurance-publications/~/media/481bd2be6ac7414cb4248996d259 f8f5.ashx Accessed December 2017.

24 Myers, L., A., Walton, S., M., and Mason, G., 2014, 'Does Big 4 consulting impair audit quality', Paper, Timothy Seidel School of Accountancy, John M. Huntsman School of Business, Utah State University, August 2014. Available at: https://busi ness.illinois.edu/accountancy/wp-content/uploads/sites/12/2014/09/Audit- Symposium-Session-V-Lisic-Myers-Pawlewicz-Seidel.pdf https://business.lsu.

edu/Accounting/Documents/Seminar%20Series/Linda%20Myers.pdf Accessed December 2017.

25 Xie, F., 2016, 'Competition, auditor independence and audit quality', PhD thesis. *University of Hawaii*. December 2016. Available at: https://scholarspace. manoa.hawaii.edu/bitstream/10125/51624/1/2016-12-phd-xie.pdf Accessed January 2018.

26 Kowaleski, Z. T., Mayhew, B. W., and Tegeler, A. C., 2018, 'The impact of consulting services on audit quality: An experimental approach', *Journal of Accounting Research*, January 2018. Available at: https://onlinelibrary.wiley.com/doi/abs/10.1111/1475-679X.12197 Accessed May 2018.

27 King, I., 2018, 'Mergers may hold the answer to challenging the Big Four auditors', *The Times*, 31 July 2018.

28 Ibid.

29 Ibid.

30 Marriage, M., and Ford, J., 2018, 'Auditors propose temporary client cap for Big Four: concession by industry aimed at staving off UK competition investigation', *Financial Times*, 24 August 2018. Available at: www.ft.com/content/8ade6fa4-a787-11e8-8ecf-a7ae1beff35b Accessed August 2018.

31 Ibid.

32 Kinder, T., 2018, 'Bank queries appointment of Grant Thornton as Goldman auditor', *The Times*, 10 July 2018. Available at: www.thetimes.co.uk/article/bank-of-england-queries-goldman-auditor-grant-thornton-0rqxwx7dw Accessed July 2018.

33 Monaghan, A., 2018, 'Regulator urges inquiry into breaking up big four accountancy firms', *The Guardian*, 16 March 2018. Available at: www.theguardian.com/business/2018/mar/16/frc-inquiry-big-four-accountancy-kpmg-deloitte-pwc-ey Accessed April 2018.

34 The authors reserve the right to keep publish this work separately.

8   Disruptive audit structures

Further options

Appendix 1.08.1 provides a summary of the Big Four defence against a possible break-up. Appendix 1.08.2 gives a background summary of the business segmentation of the Big Four firms and how this may impact any break-up.

Have the Big Four won?

For now, the Big Four seem to have won the break-up argument – temporarily perhaps, especially after the CMA has dismissed any ideas of breaking up the Big Four. The argument for not splitting up the Big Four also draws upon benefits of deep sectoral expertise gained from a range of advisory activities and how that leads to improved audit quality. However, we have found no supporting evidence to support this proposition, though size is important. Alongside that, the Big Four also say there are the Chinese walls between audit and non-audit work within their firm that are unbreakable and that audit is completely independent and even sacrosanct.[1] Both cannot be true. That said we can see the argument that an audit team can consult their advisory colleagues for their sectoral knowledge – but only where the advisory section does NOT work with that audit client. Perhaps a moot distinction?

As we've previously noted, the Big Four have persuaded the CMA and the FRC that the break-up scenario of the Big Four is either impossible or unworkable. The situation as reported by the FT is that the CMA has given way but in return the Big Four has to come back with their own ideas. This included the BIG Four lending staff, software or expertise to their sampler rivals, and also the possibility of joint audits (discussed in Chapter 9):

> The talks came a day after industry body, the Institute of Chartered Accountants in England and Wales, met with officials at the Competition and Markets Authority to discuss a potential investigation of

the audit market. The CMA officials suggested the accounting firms should put forward their own solutions for tackling the lack of competition in the market and reduce the dominance of the Big Four.... If the firms fail to come up with viable propositions then the CMA could be forced to launch an investigation of the audit market which might result in a forced break-up of the largest firms.[2]

That said the CMA actually veered away from any confrontation with the Big Four, preferring dual audits, strengthening of the scrutiny on audit committees and peer review. None of which we think will work.

Essentially the FRC has washed its hands of any structural reform, and the CMA is not anxious to conduct another investigation. The last one was unsuccessful and even produced the opposite effect (combined with the ARD). Also a CMA investigation is likely to take a long time (years rather than months), and the CMA feels it would be very complicated. That said, the FT reported (as above) that if the Big Four fail to come up with viable propositions then the CMA could be forced to launch an investigation of the audit market. We feel that joint audits reduce audit quality (see next chapter), and that size matters so it would be impossible to build up the mid-tier firms fast enough to rectify the problem. But the Big Four might be given a temporary reprieve if they bring enough of such ideas to the fore.

Earlier it was reported by Reuters that:

> Industry officials say contact between accountants and the CMA has begun and the sector's hope is for an agreement within months to limit how many audits the Big Four can undertake and thereby head off more radical change.
>
> "If asked, the profession would be willing to work with the CMA to develop a market-led solution on how to get from four to more", said David Barnes, Deloitte's global public policy partner.[3]

Apart from joint audits and lending resources to the mid-tier firms, there may be other factors at play, for example:

1) Another big failure of similar size and impact to Carillion could cause a re-evaluation of all alternatives. Or the tipping point may be several smaller failures of the size of SIG or Conviviality, or several failures similar to BHS, which is highly likely given that the retail sector is particularly susceptible to disruption.

2) The audit market is running out of large audit firms without any conflict of interest. The mid-tier firms do not have the requisite size, prestige, global reach or experience. As our own research has shown,

this is an iron-clad view. As of 2018, these companies have or had run out of choice.

a)   Carillion used all four of the Big Four and had no degree of freedom in choice for the next auditor.
b)   When Vodafone was short of options, it told EY, Deloitte and KPMG to free themselves from potential conflicts that would prevent them from tendering for the role of its next auditor.
c)   Goldman Sachs also uses all of the Big Four and its dilemma has been noted:

> Goldman, which is audited by PWC globally, is understood to have looked outside the Big Four for its UK auditor because of its existing non-audit contracts with KPMG, Deloitte and EY, which provide services such as consulting to the bank. Goldman has used PWC as its auditor since 1926 and paid it more than $50 million in 2016.[4]

See Appendix 1.08.3 for a consideration of the number of UK banks or subsidiaries that need to be audited and how the Big Four have to divide themselves among all of these for both audit and consultancy work. Normally, a client would not want their auditor to also audit or undertake substantial additional tasks. There are simply not enough of the Big Four to complete the audit and consultancy tasks. We'll call this the 'insufficient number' problem.

If another big failure can be regarded as a punch to the audit markets, it is the constant drip-drip-drip of the 'insufficient number' problem that is eroding the credibility of the Big Four in the audit market. That is of more immediate importance and may be the ultimate factor in forcing an increase in the number of audit firms by splitting the Big Four in some way. The Big Four may not like this, but it's their success and prestige which has sown the seeds of their downfall – ironically, not a failure at all but their glorious success. That success will mean some form of break-up – either voluntarily or by edict – in order that there are enough suitable firms to be shared by all that require their services. So the audit only and other possibilities that we discussed previously may still be a viable possibility. If not the short-run then the long-run.

The joint audits (Big Four plus a mid-tier firm [see next chapter]) reduce audit quality and increase audit costs. So that option is not so workable. And the Big Four lending resources initiative to the mid-tier firms still conflicts with one of our four axioms: the axiom of size matters and is linked to audit quality.[5] Interestingly the argument went that the

Big Four each had spent hundreds of millions of pounds on technology in recent years and if the Big Four were to share personnel and allow access to the same technology that could bring about change for the mid-tier firms. Though we doubt that this would make much difference – the axiom is too well embedded in reality and in beliefs.[6] So if these Big Four solutions that might be put forward do not work, or are seen to not be working, then we are back to square one.

Splitting the Big Four into audit-only and consultancy firms

As we've argued that the failure of the Big Four suggested solutions, 'another big failure' and/or 'insufficient number' problems remain a threat to the status quo.

Ignoring the international network issue for the moment, the argument goes that splitting up the Big Four into audit-only and consultancy firms would, in theory, increase competition and reduce conflicts of interest in the sector. This would be a once-and-for-all change that would solve the problem. Note that GT recently said they would not compete in the listed company market in the UK (their Irish counterpart took a different view in the Irish market). That still leaves BDO of the mid-tier firms but their share is pitifully small (and we think likely to decline further).

The FRC (in principle), the government (reluctantly), a string of academics, even one of our author team (John) all think that audit only is a good idea. Krish and Rod are against breaking the Big Four because of the knock-on network implications. However, it would provide more freedom of choice. Freedom of choice or the number of firms that a PIE can ask to tender for an audit is important.

Several comments made to us by Big Four partners and others indicated the general sentiment that the break-up movement currently seems unstoppable but that they would try to avoid it. For now, they seem to have succeeded, although the issues of 'another big failure' and 'insufficient numbers' discussed earlier still remain.

Let us imagine an alternative reality. Another failure of the magnitude of Carillion has occurred and everyone agrees that despite the objections of the Big Four, something has to be done. If the 'audit-only' option is implemented, what will the 'audit-only entity' consist of? Table 8.1 shows a breakdown of KPMG's activities. This is interesting because it provides a split into divisions or segments, which allows us a glimpse of what an audit-only firm might look like.

In 2018, KPMG had the poorest of reputations and they jumped first, leading to no non-audit work for the FTSE 350 audit clients. This is new and goes beyond the 70% cap. Later PwC and EY joined forces with KPMG to ban non-audit work for the larger audit clients. However, it forces the displaced consultancy (non-audit work) to the remaining Big Four firms which consequently increases the 'insufficient number' problem.

Audit-only size

The audit-only part of the firm could be separated out maybe with some extra resources to cope with the audit add-ons that usually rise. So small parts of the activities under the headings of Deal Advisory, Risk Consulting and Management Consulting could be combined with Audit only – allowing the Audit-only firms to undertake the vital audit add-ons (within the 70% non-audit cap and blacklisted items). However, the vast majority of the Deal Advisory, Risk Consulting and Management Consulting would form the Consulting unit.

So Audit would be a little more than the division as it is currently (plus some additional resources to deal with audit add-ons) as defined above. There would need to be some division of the buildings, central costs and IT systems. The audit-only division of each of the Big Four would be smaller. Less than one-third or one-quarter of current fee income; perhaps little more in staff numbers representing the manual nature of some audit work and less than one-fifth of the total assets. Hence the audit-only firms would be much smaller than the large organizations they came from.

The degree of freedom and increased choice

To summarize our discussion from Chapter 7, our best estimate was that the degree of freedom of choice, after extensive modelling, would increase by a factor very close to or over 100% of the current choice.[7]

The audit-only firm would be unfettered by conflicts of interest with the consulting firm. Either by design or by regulation, the audit division could be made to do just statutory audit work (with small audit add-ons), but without many of the substantial additional add-ons which would have to be farmed out to one of the other Big Four consulting divisions. There would be total separation between the audit-only and the consulting firm. In fact it may be necessary to make this type of name change unacceptable:

PwC Audit   PwC Consulting

What might have to be enforced in more of an Arthur Andersen and Accenture name split:

PwC Audit   Coopers and Price Consulting

If you allowed too many other functions to top-up the audit-only division, then you once again come into a conflict of interest situation. There would have to be hard limits. This might be statutory audit only plus in its most rigid form (i.e. no audit add-ons allowed), or it might be audit only plus 10%, or expanded to include the operation of the accounting system, and may be a few other areas for example. This would need to be determined. The purists would want the strictest definition of audit only.

But this means that the consulting divisions would also have to have an accounting function covering internal controls, perhaps an internal auditing service, annual report preparation and a full tax service. So the consulting division would have some audit and accounting functions. This would be a duplication of resources. But that is secondary to the separation and conflict of interest argument in this scenario. It means a measure of inefficiency but that is not at the top of the agenda in this option.

The audit-only firms could not take on other major non-audit work. This change alone would provide more choice as the blacklist and non-audit fee cap may no longer apply to the separated consulting divisions. So when it comes to an audit tender, apart from one of the Big Four who is the current auditor, it would allow all the three other of the Big Four to tender.

This would mean that there would always be at least three other audit firms who could tender which represents an increase of 100% in the freedom of choice over the current situation – assuming one of the Big Four is auditor and one acts as a consultant. But frequently three or even four of the Big Four are being used by one of the PIEs (as with Carillion).

The break-up of the Big Four might not be such a penalty to them as imagined. The consulting part of the audit firm, now separated, could indeed indulge in the blacklist work and have no cap on non-audit fees, so consulting work could be accepted without limit and without breaking any regulations.

The consulting part of the Big Four may welcome the split of audit only. They are less constrained by their audit division's conflicts of interest. They can see fines increasing which reduces overall partners' fees. They also have higher margin work which means higher fees per partner when the lower margin audit partners are hived off.

Would there be loyalty between the old ex-audit only and the now separated consulting division? Maybe but staff turnover would soon see, we think, a level playing field with the old ties gradually being whittled down.

New entrants

In terms of the possibility of new entrants into the audit market, there are a few distinct possibilities as well as some less likely scenarios. Arguably it would be difficult if not impossible because of the enormous barriers to entry. These would include the costs of having the requisite expertise, training, experience, IT systems as well as a global reach for data, expertise and comparisons. Furthermore, the international network of the Big Four is critical in today's interconnected world. In the previous chapter we proposed removing barriers of entry as a solution, but the issue once more is size equals quality. The audit market needs new entrants but they need to grow to the size and prestige of the Big Four which is an almost impossible notion. A consulting firm such as McKinsey might have the prestige if not the experience to break into audit market (but realistically it's very unlikely to try).

Distinctive possibilities even if probability is small

1) Sustainability and environmental auditing. Green and environmental areas, including externalities may give rise to a few niche consulting firms. One firm that has already established itself in this position is ERM (Environmental Resources Management; www.erm.com). Another lesser known is Southwest Environment.[8] Also AECOM Global EHS Management.[9] There are others, and new entrants can establish themselves in this new and growing sector. We expect some of the Big Four to use these specialists as a part of their overall audit programme in the future.

2) Merging the smaller firms. If the three largest mid-tier firms, GT, BDO and RSM, were to merge they would still be smaller than EY (the smallest of the Big Four in the UK) but they might make a viable fifth in a possible Big Five. We think this is unrealistic because their cultures are so different among other issues.

3) Alternatively, take one of the mid-tier firms and combine with ten or 20 of the smaller firms to create a sizeable entity. Realistically there is zero chance that this is feasible. The structure of the resulting combined firm would never be cohesive and the cultural differences would probably be too large to bridge.

4) Developing the mid-tier firms. As we discussed in Chapter 7, we can then draw upon the concept of 'Developing the mid-tier firms'. The government (via the CMA) could help by saying that the Big Four at the end of their rotation period were not all eligible for the AIM market companies and perhaps some of the private companies. By segmenting the market through CMA edict and perhaps with the help of an Act of Parliament and enhanced FRC rules, a fifth firm could have a chance to bid and win tenders. Such help has been currently rejected by the CMA.

If necessary, the Big Four might be forced to subsidize the tender process for a mid-tier firm (about £500,000 with inflation and expansion of audit scope)[10] as well as accepting some changes suggested here and any relevant recommendations from the Kingman Report that are adopted by the FRC replacement ARGA.

Remote possibilities

1) **The lawyers.** TSB called in the legal firm Slaughter and May to investigate the problems in their banking shutdown[11] (this is work that would be standard fare for one of the Big Four). Many legal firms have been eager to expand as legal budgets and fees have more than halved since the financial crisis. We regard this as a remote possibility but we would not put it past them. Clifford Chance, Linklaters or Allen & Overy, all with turnovers close to or exceeding £1.5 billion, could feasibly launch into either a niche audit market or go for a full auditing service, perhaps for certain types of companies.

2) **The consulting firms.** McKinsey, Boston, Accenture or Booz Allen may also like the idea of taking on an accounting and auditing division. This could be through organic growth, but more likely through taking over one of the mid-tier or smaller audit firms. The learning curve would be costly but they have the expertise and resources and their brands are globally well known and respected.

Table 8.1 The ten largest consulting firms in the world

	Revenue in 2016/17 $m	Revenue growth %	Market shares
Accenture	$34,850	6%	23%
PwC	$15,963	5%	11%
Deloitte	$15,360	8%	10%
EY	$14,537	11%	10%
KPMG	$11,545	6%	8%
McKinsey	$8,800	1%	5%
Boston Consulting Group	$5,600	12%	3%
Bain & Company	$4,500	10%	2%
Booz Allen Hamilton	$2,345	10%	2%

Source: Modified from www.consultancy.uk/news/14018/the-10-largest-consulting-firms-in-the-world

Finally, we take a wild leap in the dark. Who else could spend enough to overcome the barriers to entry, understand IT systems and who might create advantage by exploiting smart AI software?

1) The older software companies such as IBM, Microsoft, Oracle, SAP, Tata, Tencent, Baidu and so on.
2) The FAANG group (Facebook, Apple, Amazon, Netflix and Google/ Alphabet).
3) Large traditional companies that might want to diversify such as Walmart, Shell, Berkshire Hathaway, Exxon Mobil.
4) Car companies and electronics companies.

Whilst we acknowledge the possibility of 1) and 2) entering part of the audit market albeit at the limit of probability, we think 3) and 4) are not feasible.

Notes

1 Laurance, B., 2018, 'Crunch time for the Big Four bean counters: The account-ancy giants that keep a stranglehold on auditing are in the line of fire', *The Sunday Times*, 19 August 2018. Available at: www.thetimes.co.uk/article/crunch-time-for-the-big-four-bean-counters-td6zlwjq3 Accessed August 2018.
2 Marriage, M., 2018, 'Biggest UK auditors hold secret talks to avert watchdog probe: Firms meet in private amid fears investigation could lead to break-up of Big Four', *Financial Times*, 13 July 2018. Available at: www.ft.com/content/0605c1d8-86bc-11e8-96dd-fa565ec55929 Accessed July 2018.
3 Jones, H., 2018, 'Big Four accountants counting on capped market share to avoid break-up', *Reuters*, 1 June 2018. Available at: www.reuters.com/article/britain-accounts-regulator/big-four-accountants-counting-on-capped-market-share-to-avoid-break-up-idUSL8N1TH349 Accessed July 2018.
4 Kinder, T., 2018, 'EY wants conflict of interest waivers', *The Sunday Times*, 7 July 2018. Available at: www.thetimes.co.uk/article/ey-wants-conflict-of-inter est-waivers-9vqrc889w Accessed July 2018.
5 Size means global reach, widespread industry and sector experience and data, knowledge and prestige. In the *Financial Times* 2018 Marriage article, some execu-tives from the mid-tier accounting firms described the lending of resources offer of aid from larger rivals as condescending. Others seemed to be more open.
6 This argument was reported in the *Financial Times*, Marriage, 'Biggest UK audi-tors hold secret talks to avert watchdog probe: Firms meet in private amid fears investigation could lead to break-up of Big Four'.
7 The authors reserve the right to publish this work separately.
8 See the Southwest Environmental Limited website. Available at: www.southwest-environmental.co.uk Accessed July 2018.
9 See the AECOM website. Available at: www.aecom.com/services/environmen tal-services/ehs-management-consulting-compliance/ Accessed July 2018.

10 In 2018 the mid-tier firm GT (Grant Thornton) said this was the average cost of a tender but there is inflation and we think the scope and depth of the audit will be expanded. So £500,000 is a fair estimate for 2019 to 2021 time frame.

11 Ward, A., 2018, 'TSB calls in Slaughter and May for investigation into online banking shutdown: Magic circle firm to carry out independent probe of IT crisis', *Legal Week*, 2 May 2018. Available at: www.legalweek.com/2018/05/02/tsb-calls-in-slaughter-and-may-for-investigation-into-online-banking-shutdown/?sl return=20180403232623 Accessed July 2018.

9   Disruptive audit structures

Radical solutions

Radical alternatives to the audit market

In this chapter, we collate all the possible solutions and scenarios, even the wilder ones, and tackle each of these in turn, indicating how viable we think these solutions are. Some have been well debated, others are more 'blue-sky' solutions. We won't discuss possible solutions involving the sharing of resources with the mid-tiers firms as that has been covered in Chapters 7 and 8. (Of course the mid-tier firms may have no appetite for any help from the Big Four and their clients may not be that keen either.)

The mid-tier firms may not play ball even if the Big Four would be willing to impose (or have imposed) limits or caps on the number of listed audit clients the Big Four can have. As discussed this might be part of a deal to stave off a second formal competition review and possible break-up of themselves. Of course capping who can use the Big Four for audit brings its own problems. Anyone not obtaining the Big Four audit services would be relegated to a second division by the stock markets. Share values could depend on having a Big Four and first division auditor. Still it should not be ruled out.

1) Audit-only and consultancy split

As we discussed previously, to date the Big Four may have succeeded in persuading the authorities that this is unworkable. However, if another Carillion type failure occurs then this option may return. (See Appendix 1.09.01 for consideration of the Big Four audit-only proposals.)

2) Conflict of interest waivers

Conflict of interest waivers would allow Big Four firms to take on audit contracts even if they have a conflict of interest. This was reported by the *Times* as an EY concept:

Vodafone told EY, Deloitte and KPMG to free themselves from potential conflicts that would prevent them pitching for the role of its next auditor. EY has asked regulators to introduce emergency waivers that would allow Big Four firms to take on audit contracts even if they have a conflict of interest. Executives at the accountant have called for the introduction of waivers ahead of Vodafone's annual meeting this month when the telecoms group may be forced to tender its multimillion-pound audit contract with PwC.[1]

The Vodafone case was initially described in Chapter 8. We have also discussed Carillion's similar lack of choice and Goldman Sachs's. Another Vodafone type case cropped up with SIG (a FTSE 250 company and also subject to an FRC review – discussed in detail in the series volume *Financial Failures and Corporate Scandals: From Enron to Carillion*). Only one Big Four firm was eligible to bid for the role of auditor to the SIG in 2018 as the other firms were ruled out due to existing work and conflicts of interest. The issue of lack of choice among the Big Four increases concerns about the concentration in the UK audit market.

EY's head of UK audit addressed this in the context of the Kingman Review:

> "The rules have created a challenge for companies who have not actively managed their tender process to ensure that potential auditors do not have non-audit conflicts", Hywel Ball, head of UK audit at EY, said. "One solution could be to give the regulator the ability to introduce emergency waivers, in exceptional circumstances, which would provide companies with greater choice when selecting their auditor." Mr Ball said EY had asked Sir John Kingman to consider conflict waivers as part of his "root and branch" review of the Financial Reporting Council, which regulates auditors.[2]

Viability verdict: it still does not provide a solution to the 'insufficient numbers' problem. Moreover, not everyone is happy with his suggestion. One commentator opined:

> They must be joking. They betray (sic) a massive sense of entitlement in making that request, especially after a year when quality and reliability of an increasing number audit reports are rightly being questioned.[3]

3) Relaxation of the blacklist to exclude tax and valuation services

There is a precedent for relaxing the blacklist: Belgium exercised the option (under the EU directive) to allow the provision of tax and valuation services. So if the UK were to allow tax and valuation services to the audits firm, this would allow a greater degree of freedom. Modelling this (discussed in Chapter 8) indicates that this might work. However there are still two reservations with this solution:

1) The rationale for the blacklist was to increase auditor independence. We know that greater independence is associated with higher quality audits. So given the FRC's current concerns about current low quality audits, we cannot see the current reviews or anyone else rushing to adopt this scenario. But it still remains an option and a better one than just introducing the waiver option in terms of choice. That is because all PIEs require audit and tax advice (especially if the companies have subsidiaries in the EU and globally).
2) There are insufficient Big Four companies to offer sufficient choice, as the Bank of England concurs:

> The Bank of England said on Wednesday [July 2018] there is too little choice of auditor for big banks who must switch bookkeepers under European Union rules.[4]

We believe that the Bank of England is saying there should be more choice. Four firms is just too few. In the evidence we collected, this view is echoed by others. Although we did not collect specific evidence on this issue, we believe that there is a widespread view that 'Four' is too few. Moreover, the mid-tier firms do not have the global reach, experience or sufficient prestige, and hence the Bank of England does not accept the mid-tier firms as viable contenders to audit a large bank.[5] Even resource sharing with the Big Four would not be a sufficient change. As we have said, growing the mid-tier or challenger firms, to be equivalent to the Big Four would take a decade or two but we doubt that it would be possible - the Big Four are also growing apace.

   Viability verdict: Conflict of interest would help the numbers/choice issue but relaxation of blacklist would be better, although that has independence issues. Though as before it is not an enduring solution to the 'insufficient numbers' problem.

4) Allow auditors to be sued and 5) make insurance mandatory

In the US, there is a whole, industry dedicated to suing auditors and the companies involved. There, any shareholder can make a claim which will be supported by a representative plaintiff in a class action. The litigation after the pyramid scheme of Bernie Madoff[6] addressed this aspect at length. There have been at least nine settlements in excess of $1 billion:

- Enron in 2007 ($7.2 billion);
- WorldCom in 2005 ($6.2 billion);
- Cendant in 2000 ($3.3 billion);
- Tyco in 2007 ($3.2 billion);
- AOL Time Warner in 2006 ($2.5 billion);
- Nortel Networks in 2006 ($1.1 billion).

Note that some of these settlement sums include the overall settlements against all parties, not only the auditor.

Currently (2018 to 2020) there is an increase in merger and acquisition activity. This often leads to parties suing because the companies being bought do not measure up to the buyers' expectations. Hence court actions often follow the takeover activity. The US tech company HP is suing the previous management of Autonomy plc who allegedly inflated their value during the sale to HP. There was also some talk of suing the UK auditors, Deloitte. This case is ongoing.[7] PwC may be sued following the various court judgements in the Colonial Bank case discussed earlier. These and other cases are analyzed in detail in the companion volume in this series, *Financial Failures and Corporate Scandals: From Enron to Carillion.*

The banning of non-audit work for audit clients is discussed in Appendix 1.09.1

UK auditors' liability

In the UK, the pivotal case which set the precedent was the Caparo judgement. This overturned the previous assumption of the responsibility of auditors to the shareholders of a company and the public to ensure that the accounts of a company could be depended upon. The judgement seemed to rely on the fact the auditors had no contractual relationship with shareholders but only with the company who appoints them. Two subsequent cases modified this decision somewhat. The current situation is unclear. It remains more difficult to bring a claim against auditors in the UK than it is in the US. Auditor Liability Limitation Agreements (LLAs) could limit liability but they are not adopted in practice. The agreements require shareholder approval – and they seldom agree.

The upshot seems to be that in the UK, the Caparo precedent still restricts claims brought against the auditors as a whole, though there are many complex aspects.[8] In theory, an auditor can be sued, although it may be costly. But is not the auditor's job to provide a guarantee of the company's continued existence or the prevention of fraud. The auditor can claim that they did everything under law and guidelines and that their audit confirmed a true and fair view, i.e. they fulfilled all their responsibilities and the attitude seems to be 'prove otherwise'. The US adopts a slightly different position which is more kind to the claimant. Our opinion is that the basic law on auditor's liability needs to change to allow litigation to be easier and possible – but within certain limits.

Prospectuses are subject to a different set of rules regarding litigation. In a £200m claim[9] against RBS, a group of shareholders alleged they had been misled about the bank's financial health when it launched a £12 billion rights issue in 2008. This is a claim by a discrete group of shareholders and seems to be a claim under the Financial Services and Markets Act 2000 (FSMA).[10]

Roger Lawson[11] puts the current legal position into sharp and somewhat critical focus:

> This judgement [the Caparo case] made it exceedingly difficult for shareholders to pursue auditors, and although there are possible 'derivative' actions there are other obstacles that have been introduced over the years that reduce the potential liability of auditors. One is that they are now mostly not simple partnerships with the partners being individually and personally liable, but Limited Liability Partnerships (LLP). Secondly auditors write their contracts with companies and these now limit the scope of liability substantially – they frequently exclude liability for omissions that one would expect auditors to identify.
>
> With the declining quality of audits, and the lack of competition between the big four audit firms, it is surely time to revisit the whole legal framework under which auditors operate. With companies often more interested in reducing audit costs than ensuring the accounts can be relied upon, one can see why and how the standard has been reduced over the years.

One of Lawson's suggestions is the use of standardized contracts between auditors and companies. These would be based on 'model' contracts as laid down by the FRC or the FCA/PRA, and drawn up based on the advice of investors, as well as stakeholders. Public interest could be added as a rightful concern.

One auditor we interviewed said:

> Standardised contracts are interesting. Bear in mind the scope and duties are already defined in the Companies Act and ISAs. Quite a

bit of what Lawson says about excluding liability may apply to non-statutory work – [but] there is very little scope in relation to statutory audits.

That seems to make a case for expanding what should be included in the statutory audit. We discuss this in detail in the series volume *Disruption in Auditing*.

Liability capped?

Should the amount an audit firm is liable for be limited or capped in some way? The most likely outcome would be that if auditors could be sued then the audit firms would seek insurance cover against such eventualities. Professional indemnity insurance is already taken out by audit firms' individual senior staff (similar to medical doctors) – claims are thereby paid by the insurance company.

Once some sort of litigation becomes a realistic possibility in the UK, then it is likely (as in all professions) that there would be insurance policies both singly for a professional (already in place) and for the firm. So suing auditors as a solution means insurance policies which adds cost and may take away some motivation for improved audit quality. To ban insurance and impose stronger caps on litigation might improve the motivational aspect. A better solution might be to have some form of excess.

The net effect for the auditing firms would be increased premiums to cover themselves professionally, and they wouldn't really be affected other than their profits would be reduced by the amount of the insurance premium (it would be more problematic if they could not obtain cover at an acceptable price). If premiums increased based on the FRC's AQR survey, this might act as an added incentive to quality.

We can see an example of this in action in Germany which has liability for auditors although there is a cap unless gross negligence is proven. The limit is €1 million except for companies whose shares trade on regulated markets where the cap limit is €4 million.[12] Could such a limit be agreed upon in the UK? While, in theory, a limit might be agreed, it might never happen because neither the company directors nor the shareholders would find this in their best interests. If this ever became a reality, it would need some sort of legislation to put a cap on the amount that could be awarded. We think this should be higher than the German limit, and should be split between the offending parties as awarded by a court.

The impact of the civil financial settlements paid out by auditors may or may not be a financial burden. But there is also an impact on behaviour – and that should not be underestimated. This might suggest that it should be easier to make civil financial settlements. This might require new legislation and new powers to remove any ambiguities. Additionally, we think that there should be a new set of rules and regulations, and a change in corporate law.

The viability verdict on the solution of suing the auditors is:

- Litigation with or without some sort of limit or insurance is a potential possibility as part or all of an overall solution. To counter the motivational aspect the audit firm may have an excess and have to pay the first £x million of any claim (just as with car insurance). Insurance claims should be limited at, say, triple the level of the maximum FRC fine (this would rarely be 100% the fault of the auditor). This may cause a clash with FRC fines as doubling up on penalties and punishments. However, in practical terms, we think that all concerned would probably want FRC fines or US style liability but not both.
- Probably unacceptable to the audit industry.

6) Audit guarantees

The three of us have given some further thought to the concept of an audit guarantee. We think that the first thing that needs to be settled is for whose benefit is the guarantee to be provided? The present legal position is that the audit is undertaken for the benefit of the current shareholders. We believe that this is far too narrow a group, but let's consider the implications for this very narrow group. In the case of Enron, presumably the shareholders could claim that they had suffered a loss as a consequence of Enron's false accounts. There are lots of problems in attempting to quantify this loss, but one possible figure could be the actual fall in the value of Enron's shares when it announced that previous profits had been overstated. In today's terms, the total fall in Enron's share market value must have been several tens of billions of dollars, which might wipe out an audit firm – as was the result for Arthur Andersen. One experienced auditor commented:

> We cannot see that any accountancy firm could possibly meet such a claim and surely no insurance company would provide cover for such a potentially huge liability. Note this is assuming that it is a very narrow group (the company's shareholders) who are claiming damages.

On the other hand, BP and VW have survived fines and settlements of tens of billions of dollars, so we could see that this is worth considering. But firstly, we started to react against the idea of guarantees: what would be the point of making the auditor guarantee their audit?

Two rather different objectives can be envisaged:

1) to motivate the auditor to be more careful and conscientious in his or her audit;
2) to transfer risk from the company to the auditor.

One auditor commented:

> One might say the old pre LLP regime with unlimited liability focussed the mind rather more than the present position. Today naming the partner who signs the report has a similar effect. He/she does face difficulty in being accepted as lead auditor by other companies in circumstances where past work is being investigated let alone that investigation being concluded – that helps to focus the mind.

And transferring the risk could mean that the company's management would be less motivated to prepare accurate accounts.

The whole issue is fraught with contradictions. We cannot see how a guarantee could be made operational: either the auditor would seek to avoid liability by reporting an unrealistically wide range for profit, or the auditor would charge an astronomical fee for his or her services (or could never complete the work). We suspect that the problem is that a guarantee is essentially the equivalent of insurance and that the accounts are not a suitable subject for insurance because, in the present state of human knowledge, they are too imprecise. As with the insurance option, maybe the guarantee would have to have an excess in order to mitigate any motivational effects from having reduced risk.

One experienced auditor raised the question of meaning:

> What does 'guaranteeing the audit' mean? How is it different from the present opinion – is it saying I guarantee the company will still be in business? That would be unreasonable. The auditor is not an insurer.

Initially, we were keen the idea of some sort of guarantee. But the idea was severely criticized by several commentators and auditors who argued that audit guarantees were unworkable. The argument goes that such guarantees cannot be applied to a business which only claims to give reasonable (not absolute) assurance and does so using techniques which are permeated by judgement – a recurring amorphous concept. The other issue is that auditors believe that the resulting rules and regulations would make the audit role very unattractive for the individual professionals involved.

We think the only answer would be to limit the guaranteed amount any court award and/or settlement, and specifically the portion awarded against the auditor. In order to mitigate motivational aspects, there should be an excess so that the audit firm would pay the first £x of any claim.

The viability verdict is therefore:

- In essence the guarantee is very similar in practice to an insurance policy with similar limitations. We found that there was not much enthusiasm to go down this route.
- Probably unacceptable to the audit industry.

7) Auditor's independence

Concerns about independence and audit quality have been at the root of many of the complaints we have discussed. Axiom 4 from Chapter 7 states that 'Greater independence leads to higher audit quality'. So greater independence becomes a goal in achieving higher audit quality. In narrow terms, the solution is to split the consulting division from the audit division. But this does not provide a large step in auditor independence. However, there are two other possible ways in which independence can be established.

1) Sever the money link between the company being audited and the auditor and the means of some type of scale fees.
2) Remove the choice of who is appointed from the company being audited and give it to some third party.

We have seen that there is a close relationship between the entity being audited and the auditor. In fact, we claimed that the tendering process brought in by mandatory rotation has ushered in a closer relationship. In Chapter 7, we showed how the senior management of the entity being audited (often) make their judgements based on who they get along with, and are most comfortable, while the external auditors know that their fees depend in part on the recommendations of those managers.

It is widely understood that for a professional accountant to be capable of exercising the function of auditor, it is vital that he/she be independent of that firm's management. This point is evidenced by the provisions for non-audit work in both the Sarbanes-Oxley Act, EU directive and as interpreted by the FRC. But this has not ensured independence.

So we turn to how the auditor should be appointed. There are several possibilities:

1) The FRC or some regulatory body chooses the auditor. This may be coupled with payment being made by the state (perhaps levied from the firms being audited). This is perhaps the easiest option. But fees would also need to be set in some formulaic way[13] – and not by the firm being audited.

2) The auditor is appointed by a body that represents the shareholders. We are against this, as management usually have proxy votes to ensure their desired result. And this method would not represent all the stakeholders of the firm.

3) The auditor is appointed by a body that represents the stakeholders in general (including representatives of shareholders, employees, customers, the local community and so on). One can envisage the creation of such a body as part of a grand reform of company law, which might include the institution of two-tier boards on the German model.[14] When Theresa May became prime minister, she was in favour of more employee representation.[15]

4) The auditor is appointed by the state. There are precedents for the appointment of persons similar to auditors to be made by an organ of the state, e.g. a court of law may appoint a solicitor as a trustee for a minor. This arrangement generally works well for two reasons: there is a well-defined body of men and women from whom the trustee can be chosen, and the duties of a trustee are well defined in law. Furthermore, there are arrangements (through the disciplinary procedures of the solicitor's profession) to ensure that the trustees act in accordance with the law. In theory, both these conditions could be fulfilled for audit, although we feel that professional accountants do not (currently) have the same high reputation for integrity as solicitors.

5) The auditor is appointed by rota system, so that the next available of the Big Four was chosen as long as they did not conflict with the consulting rule. This could give rise to management being able to game the system through the judicious awarding of consulting contracts. The only way this would work is if there were much more choice.

6) The auditor is assigned randomly. Once more this would require much more choice.

How should the audit function be paid for? It seems obvious to us that the costs of the audit of a business firm should fall on that firm. But it is essential that the amount should not be fixed by the firm's management (which could compromise the auditor's independence), nor by the auditor him- or herself. The only alternative is a standard scale of charges set by the FRC or another state regulator. We believe that such a standard scale exists (or has existed in the past) for the audit of friendly societies. But there would need to be some flexibility agreed to reflect complexity or difficulty of the audit, e.g. number of subsidiaries and geographical reach of entity and the scope of events. This may in itself be a problem – it may be impossible to reach agreement.

Again, several auditors jumped on our assumptions. Typical comments include:

- Very difficult for the FRC to produce a tariff of penalties;
- Too much variation in systems and procedures both by client and our auditing processes;
- Hard to assess when the audit work process is usually entirely internal to a specific company and the systems and procedures it operates.

It is much easier for FCA/PRA to make judgements as they derive a mathematical relationship with the failure to follow a specific rule. We do not see why the FRC cannot do the same. If we are changing the functions of the FRC this could include a widening of the FRC powers – with a suitable mathematical formula.

So there are two viability verdicts from this analysis:

- A neutral third party chooses the auditor (but there may still be a tendering process, etc.).
- Scale fees plus some flexibility to reflect complexity or difficulty of the audit.

The audit industry is not going to relish the above but it is the only way to ensure a significantly greater degree of independence, and hence higher quality audits. There may be a dispute about our axiom 4 but greater independence should be a goal in itself.

8) The state runs the audit function

A major issue is the extent to which the state intervenes in the audit market. Various scenarios can be considered which differ in the degree of state involvement. In this scenario, the state employs and controls the auditors, who are in effect public servants. This was the situation with the UK's National Audit Office and with the Greek government's audit service (SOL) up to about 20 years ago. In both cases, the general view was that neither organization was efficient, but it can be argued that this was the result of negative briefing from the private audit profession. Without denying the important work that the National Audit Office currently does, we dismiss the state running the audit function as being non-workable and/or inefficient. We think that the current mixed private and public system works well.

Viability verdict: not feasible.

9) Joint audits

This possible scenario proposes pairing one of the Big Four with one of the mid-tier or smaller companies in order to increase choice and bolstering the fees of the smaller firm – strongly supported by the CMA. This might become important as this may be suggested by the Big Four as a solution to the 'insufficient numbers' issue. There are two factors to be considered: a) do joint audits result in higher audit fees (because of duplication)? And b) what is the effect on quality? One study argued against this model:

> Joint audits involve two audit firms and may have the desired effect of 'Two heads are better than one'. However, joint audits may also induce one firm to free-ride on another firm's performance and therefore damage the total precision of audit evidence. In addition, since joint audits involve two firms, it may be more expensive for the audited company to 'bribe' its auditors. However, adding another audit firm may create an 'opinion shopping' opportunity for the company, thereby threatening auditor independence.
>
> We investigate three regimes: single audits by a big firm; joint audits by two big firms; joint audits by one big firm and one small firm. We compare the three regimes along three dimensions: total audit evidence precision; auditor independence; and total audit fee. Our analysis suggests that auditor independence is more likely to be compromised under joint audits. Moreover, joint audits involving a technologically inefficient firm (a small firm) may impair audit quality since a free-riding problem would prevail and result in lower total audit evidence precision.[16]

This study has been supported by other studies. For example:[17]

> What the research does show unequivocally, however, is that joint audits cost significantly more than single firm audits. Audit fees are

higher in France than in both the UK and Italy, an unexpected finding based on the relative strength of the three legal regimes. With many other factors controlled for, it seems highly likely that higher costs are due to the joint audit requirement.

However, an examination of the earnings management data suggests the higher audit fees observed in France are not associated with higher audit quality. In summary, a) joint audits are associated with higher audit fees, and b) may be lower audit quality[18] though this is not fully proven.

Viability verdict: joint audits appear to have higher costs and no perceivable improvement in audit quality. That is likely to be true for the Big Four plus smaller firm models so which may not be a feasible scenario in the UK. This is important as the CMA has suggested this as a possible solution.

11) The raw data and self-service auditing scenario

As one senior auditor said:

> In my mind, the only way to break that 'public perception gap' problem is to give users access to authenticated data and let them build their own models. Most of the expectation gap problems stem from having to deal with inter period allocations of various historical cash flows. Take away the requirement for accounting periods and provide up-to-date authenticated data and the problem is dissipated.

However, present UK law[19] states that only members of recognized bodies may carry out audits – that is presently the case for the named person signing the audit opinion (on the Annual Report). This makes it impossible for anybody to do self-service audits. Moreover, the high-profile scandals around misuse of data is a critical issue and GDPR[20] has since brought things into sharper focus.

Viability verdict: This changing public concern may be a strong limiting factor and this scenario may fail simply on the basis of privacy concerns.

12) Levelling the playing field between big and small firms

In Chapter 6, we introduced the theme that machine learning systems as currently being developed will be able to learn most of the auditing functions and to (eventually) undertake them with little human input.

More importantly, a standard audit AI system would be available not just to the Big Four but to a wider set of accounting firms, or even new entrants to the auditing market. It is possible that the major part of such a system would be open source. Such operations would require staff with experience and expertise of AI (with a knowledge of TensorFlow[21]) and with a measure of auditing knowledge and expertise. Such systems would be able to draw upon a global experience and have a global reach for experience and data. It would be as if a user had a large high-powered office everywhere in the world. Once developed, such audit AI systems would mean that the Big Four might lose their advantage – smaller accounting firms could operate in the same way with all the advantages and resources of the Big Four.

We take the view that there will still be a role for the human auditor. With more data at their fingertips, auditors can move to higher-value analysis, including forward scenario planning. The end result could be an improvement in the quality of the audit, and more importantly, increased confidence on the part of investors and stakeholders.[22]

Viability verdict: Depends on technological advances and likely to be some distance into the future. May become a solution in the 2035 plus time frame.

13) AI creates auditing market solution

There is one last solution we are going to propose that is at the limits of current thinking, but is nevertheless feasible given the rate of technological development. The following example is a useful analogue.

The Chinese Foxconn group has a global stranglehold over the consumer electronics and smartphone production. But the major marketing and R & D is undertaken by Apple, Hyundai and others. The Italian group Luxottica occupies the same position in sunglasses manufacturing; their brands include Ray-Ban and most European luxury and fashion brands. No one grumbles because they are sold and distributed through multiple well-known brands. In both cases, the dominance is hidden because pricing, functionality and style are set by the individual brands.

These examples provide a clue to one possible solution to the structure of the auditing sector. Imagine the existence of one universal, anonymous AI auditing engine, perhaps created by Google's Deep Mind, which is controlled and sold through multiple brands such as the Big Four. They would personalize the front end, adding their own functionality, style and price. There would be no competition on the basis of scale because the single auditing engine would be used globally and have global reach – far in excess of the current Big Four's abilities. There could be a fixed sliding scale of fees (depending on complexity) for the audit engine, and a competitive portion for the marketing and management function and front end. However, the basic standards, rules and regulations, statistical criteria and tests, including the scope and depth of the audit, would be laid down by a body such as the FRC, maybe in conjunction with the international bodies of IFAC and the IAASB to reflect the global nature of the clients, and the US regulatory authorities may have a significant oversight over the US rules and standards. There may need to be slight tailoring (already built-in and/or updated) for each country, or it may be that the FRC or equivalent would run and maintain the UK audit AI engines though each of the Big Four and any others would be free to customize their front end and any bespoke tailoring features. Materiality would be governed by a similar body.

Viability verdict: this is definitely a blue-sky scenario but do not rule it out as a possible future. We are probably talking about 2035 onwards but still food for thought.

See Appendix 1.09.02 for a view of the expansion of the scope of audit for the public interest.

Notes

1 Kinder, T., 2018, 'EY wants conflict of interest waivers', *The Sunday Times*, 7 July 2018. Available at: www.thetimes.co.uk/article/ey-wants-conflict-of-inter est-waivers-9vqrc889w Accessed July 2018.

2 Ibid.

3 Ibid. in the comments section under the main article under the name 'Man on the Street'.

4 Jones, H., 2018, 'Bank of England says worried by lack of auditor choice for banks', *Reuters*, 11 July 2018. Available at: https://uk.reuters.com/article/uk-boe-banks-accounts/bank-of-england-says-worried-by-lack-of-auditor-choice-for-banks-idUKKBN1K12GN Accessed July 2018.

5 Also see: Jones, H., 2018, 'Goldman Sachs: Bank of England says worried by lack of auditor choice for banks', *4-Traders*, 11 July 2018. Available at: www.4-traders. com/GOLDMAN-SACHS-GROUP-12831/news/Goldman-Sachs-Bank-of-England-says-worried-by-lack-of-auditor-choice-for-banks-26911141/ Accessed June 2018. And see: Marriage, M, McLannahan, B., and Gray, A., 2018, 'EU rules force US banks to overhaul ties with auditors: Goldman, Citi, and Morgan Stanley among lenders that will need to alter arrangements', *Financial Times*, 16 October 2017. Available at: www.ft.com/content/e66db868-aff6-11e7-beba-5521c713abf4 Accessed June 2018.

6 A famous Ponzi scheme (money raised to be invested and repaid as interest) discovered in 2008 and involving a fraud of $65 billion. The largest in history. Available at: https://en.wikipedia.org/wiki/Madoff_investment_scandal Accessed July 2018.

7 The CFO has been found guilty in US courts. The CEO trial awaits but is likely to follow suit – as reported. See for example: Corfield, G., 2018, 'Mike Lynch's British court showdown v HPE pushed back to 2019: US corp asked for extra time to file expert witness statements', *The Register*, 9 May 2018.

8 There are many problems. See for example the synopsis and articles. But for the UK precedents, see: ACCA, 2018, 'Auditor liability', *ACCA Global Student Exam Support Resources*, 2 February 2018. Available at: www.accaglobal.com/uk/en/student/exam-support-resources/professional-exams-study-resources/p7/technical-articles/auditor-liability.html Accessed March 2018. For the US litigation and calculation of damages see: Ferrell, A., 2011, 'New insights into calculating securities damages', *The Harvard Law School Forum on Corporate Governance and Financial Regulation*, 20 June 2011. Available at: https://corpgov.law.harvard.edu/2011/06/20/new-insights-into-calculating-securities-damages/ Accessed October 2017.

9 Croft, J., 2018, 'RBS shareholders still waiting for £200m compensation: Bank had settled lawsuit almost a year ago over rescue funding', *Financial Times*, 18 March 2018. Available at: www.ft.com/content/58fa040c-284e-11e8-b27e-cc62a39d57a0 Accessed April 2018.

10 Amended over the years and now incorporating some of MiFID I & II – Markets in Financial Instruments Directive (now with version released in 2017).

11 Lawson, R., 2018, 'Audit quality and the Caparo judgement', *Roger W. Lawson's Blog: Audits, Laws & Regulations*, 7 February 2018. Available at: https://roliscon.blog/2018/02/07/audit-quality-and-the-caparo-judgement/ Accessed March 2018.

12 Dufour, A., 2014, 'Liability of statutory auditors as well as tax and legal counsels in Europe', *Association of Corporate Councils: Legal Resources*, 2 December 2014. Available at: www.acc.com/legalresources/quickcounsel/liability-of-statutory-auditors.cfm Accessed January 2016.

13 To allow for flexibility, the difficulty of the audit and the complexity of the entity being audited. Some formulaic algorithm with some manual adjustment for exceptional or one-off complexity (determined by the FRC but argued by the auditee and the auditor).

14 See this book for some more radical ideas on how to convert the corporation into a responsive 21st century organization. Mayer, C., 2013, *Firm Commitment: Why the Corporation Is Failing Us and How to Restore Trust in It*, Oxford University Press, Oxford, 2013. Available at: www.amazon.co.uk/Firm-Commitment-Corporation-Failing-Restore/dp/0198714807/ref=sr_1_1?ie=UTF8&qid=1525464240&sr=8-1&keywords=Firm+Commitment%3A+Why+The+Corporation+Is+Failing+Us+And+How+To+Restore+Trust+In+It.

15 O' Grady, F., and Bowman, S., 2017, 'Should companies be forced to put workers on boards? Was Theresa May right to U-turn on her guarantee?', *The Guardian*, 29 August 2018. Available at: www.theguardian.com/commentisfree/2017/aug/29/companies-workers-boards-theresa-may-u-turn Accessed September 2017.

16 Lu, T., and Simunic, D., A., 2012, 'Do joint audits improve or impair audit quality?', Paper. Available at: https://business.illinois.edu/accountancy/wp-content/uploads/sites/12/2014/11/Audit-2012-Deng-Lu-Simunic-Ye.pdf Accessed May 2018. And Deng, M., Lu, T., Simunic, D., A., and Ye, M., 2014, 'Do joint audits improve or impair audit quality?', *Journal of Accounting Research*, Vol. 52, No. 5, December 2014, pp. 993–1246. Available at: https://onlinelibrary.wiley.com/toc/1475679x/2014/52/5 Accessed July 2018.

17 André, P., and Schatt, A., 2017, 'Joint audits: Do they add up?', *HEC Impact: Insights from Research at HEC Lausanne, University of Lausanne*, 2 March 2017. Available at: https://wp.unil.ch/hecimpact/do-joint-audits-add-up/ Accessed July 2018. Related paper: André, P., Broye, G., Pong, C., and Schatt, Alain, 2016, 'Are joint audits associated with higher audit fees?' *European Accounting Review*, Vol. 25, No. 2, 2016, pp. 245–274. Summary and additional material can be accessed: Smith, E., 2017, 'Joint audits: Do they add up?', *Financial Director*, 23 February 2017. www.financialdirector.co.uk/2017/02/23/joint-audits-do-they-add-up/#r3z-addoor Accessed July 2018. Note that following the BT accounting scandal, Paul André and Alain Schatt of HEC Lausanne examine the impact of joint audits on costs and quality in France, Italy.

18 Although a Swedish study confirmed the increased audit fees but found higher audit quality with voluntary joint audits. Though the choice of voluntary may be a casual factor in the higher quality rating. See: Zerni, M., Haapamäki, E', Järvinen, T., and Niemi, L., 2012, 'Do joint audits improve audit quality? Evidence from voluntary joint audits', *European Accounting Review*, December 2012. Available at: www.tandfonline.com/doi/abs/10.1080/09638180.2012.678599 Accessed July 2018.

19 Criminal sanction presently exists in Companies Act. See Companies Act 2006 section 507. Available at: www.legislation.gov.uk/ukpga/2006/46/section/507 Accessed May 2018.

20 The General Data Protection Regulation (GDPR) is an EU regulation on data protection and privacy for all individuals within the European Union. It also addresses the export of personal data outside the EU. The GDPR is likely to impact smaller companies as a recent study shows that 82% of SMEs are unaware of the new legislation and will potentially be hit with large fines when it starts being enforced in 2019.

21 TensorFlow is a Google open-source software library for a range of artificial intelligence tasks and principally used in machine learning applications and neural networks.

22 EY: Building a better working world, Delaney, A., 2018, 'What is the role of the auditor in the age of AI? Let the robots process and the humans think', *Quartz*, April 2018. Available at: https://qz.com/749322/what-is-the-role-of-the-auditor-in-the-age-of-ai/ Accessed June 2018.

10 Summary and conclusions

Overview

Accountancy Magazine in July 2018 summarized their view of the current problematic state of the audit market as follows:[1]

> One in four listed audits require improvements while the Big Four's failure to challenge company managements about future forecasts and scrutinise financial decisions is undermining the value of audit, according to the latest 2017/18 Financial Reporting Council's (FRC)Audit Quality Inspections (AQI).... In the FRC's AQI report, 28% of Big Four audits were marked down as requiring improvements, with all Big Four firms performing much worse than the 2016/17 cycle when 19% of audits were pulled up for improvements. Out of 94 Big Four audits reviewed, 24 were singled out as requiring improvements with two further audits identified as requiring significant improvements. This is worse than last year when only 13 audits out of 90 required improvement, with a further two marked as requiring significant improvement.... The FRC has set a target of 90% of audits requiring no or limited improvements and this year's results highlight a sharp decline in audit quality. With only 72% hitting the acceptable standard, there are concerns about the level of trust in auditors. In 2016/17, 81% of audits were deemed to require no or only limited improvements.

Reports like these are undermining the acceptability of the current audit market. Something clearly has to change, and the finger always seems to point at some kind of reorganization of the Big Four. But as we've seen, the Big Four seem to have won the argument to avoid this so far. The CMA decided that it was reluctant to force the Big Four to spin off their audit practices calling the idea as risky of unintended consequences.

We strongly disagree that the idea is "unworkable" and disappointed that the CMA is not apparently considering any kind of break-up of the Big Four. The Big Four have yet to provide their final suggestions which we think will comprise of joint audits and the sharing of resources – both of which we feel will not have any great impact. However, there are two challenges which may force change sooner rather than later: the 'another big failure' and the 'insufficient number' issue. Despite the issues that make breaking up the Big Four a difficult solution to implement, maintaining the current status quo may only be postponing the inevitable.

Within a suitable time frame, all the radical options and solutions discussed in Chapter 9 are still possibilities. However, many of them will not be popular with the audit industry. We think that, despite any new initiatives, without radical reform, there will be financial failures of a similar order to or greater than Carillion with a similar set of circumstances (even with the IFRS 15 revenue recognition standard). In fact, in the *Disruption in Financial Reporting* volume in this series, we identify a set of firms that may be the subject of financial pressures and issues in the future – assuming nothing else changes. So the analysis of all the alternatives are still valid and will be revisited before 2025. And meanwhile, the 'insufficient number' is a pressing problem right now, and will only become greater in time. (Appendix 1.10.1 considers whether the conflict waiver will solve the insufficient numbers issue.) Kingman, in a separate letter to the Business Minster, sides more to our way of thinking than the CMA. See http://www.fin-rep.org/which-book/disruption-to-the-audit-market/

The most likely solutions and scenarios

Summary of findings so far

In previous chapters we developed the following audit quality axioms:

1) Axiom 1: size is linked to higher audit quality. Larger firms are capable of higher quality audits. See Chapter 3.
2) Axiom 2: higher audit quality is linked to shorter length of audit tenure. See Chapter 4.
3) Axiom 3: greater competition leads to better audit quality. An increase in the number of firms competing leads to higher audit quality especially in turbulent periods. See Chapter 5.
4) Axiom 4: greater independence leads to higher audit quality. See Chapter 7.

The second issue is solved by rotation. Shorter periods are better. We think this will in practice be settled at between five to seven years, and no further actions are recommended other than to retain this. (See also Appendix 1.09.1 for a further consideration of the Big Four audit-only proposal.)

Observations and recommendations

You might summarize the current insufficient numbers situation by saying that four is just a step away from no choice at all. The regulators, politicians, government, perhaps the EU, the CMA and Big Four will make their own continuing evaluations. Bringing together all the points, we make the following observations. We have tried to analyze all the alternatives neutrally. Some observations are grouped by audit market effect. The final solution may very well be a combination of these outcomes. For the moment we dismiss the CMA current conclusions as being biased, unworkable and superficial. See http://www.fin-rep.org/wp-content/uploads/book2/5-Our-response-to-the-CMA-update-paper.pdf

Addressing the 'insufficient numbers' issue:

1) **Split the Big Four into the Big Eight.** Splitting the Big Four to create the Big Eight would be messy and the international network effects make this impracticable unless mutually agreed with the US. The present organizational structure of the Big Four would be unlikely to agree to any change. Or would they? However, there would be, in practice, more choice. The Big Four have won their argument for now.

2) **Audit only.** To provide maximum flexibility the audit-only firms should be restricted to just the statutory audit (which might be expanded over the current scheme). This provides roughly 100% more choice. But how will the international networks perceive this and react – will they step in to provide the prohibited consultancy services? Three of the Big Four have agreed to audit only work for their largest clients. But banning non-audit work is entirely different from the split of a firm into separate audit-only and consultancy firms.

3) **Bolster mid-tier firms.** The aim is to incentivize the use of BDO and GT through intervention or subsidy plus Big Four help, or through the Big Four not tendering for certain types of audit or listing segment. Mazars (around the tenth largest firm) has indicated it wants to develop joint audits which should be encouraged. But size is always equated to quality so there remains a perception problem until the mid-tier grows to be large. Neither does sharing of resources with the Big Four completely solve the issue even if it worked – duplication and cultural differences mean that it is not such an immediately workable solution. The mid-tier firms will still be the second choice. This was the CMA's best remedy choice combined with joint audits to split the audit fees.

4) **Resource sharing.** As above, even if willing, it does not completely solve the problem. And the reception of the mid-tier in the clients' minds may not have changed. Why take the second tier if you can have the first tier – even if they are using the same systems?

Addressing the quality issue:

The audit-only split of the Big Four would require legislation to separate and ring-fence audit – unless achieved voluntarily as currently proposed. As indeed would the split of audit into the Big Eight. A break-up of the audit firms into the Big Eight would still have the scale and expertise that makes for an efficient audit operation. In fact it may be argued that the current size of the audit firms concentrated into just four firms are too large to be operating efficiently. There may be diseconomies of scale and the small is beautiful argument may still prevail. For example PwC offices are spread over three locations in London. Ditto Deloitte, though their main site in the city is split between several buildings. That leaves the question of whether the break-up of the Big Four into the Big Eight would help improve audit quality. Our evidence suggests that it would and the added competition would ensure a sharper response. Scale fees could counter the lower margin that competition may bring.

That leaves one issue. If the existing audit division of the Big Four in the UK is split in two, which part would remain under the group's international network umbrella? The answer is that both could report into the same international network without too many problems. There are enough anomalies around the world that this should not be an issue. Networks behave like families of practices in the same country. Problems between different country networks do not seem to deter or influence other country's networks. By and large these networks can absorb a huge shock and survive. So the network effect should not be overstated. Going back to our list of radical solutions. . . .

The FT ran a series of articles on auditing in August 2018.[2] One of these addressed the quality issue.[3] They reported a lawsuit against a Mr Mauri Botta, who worked for PwC in the US and had claimed the auditors were too close to their clients. Independence was not a factor. Mr. Botta primarily had concerns that the PwC partners were compromising their objectivity. The FT article echoed typical statements made to us by Big Four partners:

- We concentrate on building relationships and getting really close to our clients;
- No one is going to make partner unless he or she can grow revenue at a client and keep the client happy;
- Revenue growth is the key driver of our business.

This exposes a dichotomy between consulting and auditing. Auditing has a public duty element and is a check on management – the aim should not be just to please management. Auditors have a duty to other stakeholders including the shareholders. Whereas for consultancy, the sole aim is to please management and the executives commissioning the work. So there is an inherent conflict. However, when the partners are challenged on this conflict, they all back down and say a) there is no conflict, or that b) there are Chinese walls between different divisions. (See our volume *Financial Failures and Corporate Scandals: From Enron to Carillion* for indications that a) is sometimes not true and b) are rather more porous than anyone imagines.) The renewed aggressive cast of the FRC post-Carillion makes life for an auditor partner much more difficult and indeed risky. If caught, a partner's promotions prospects and that million pound salary are in jeopardy.

There is one reported fact by the same FT article which offers some hope. EY came at the bottom of the FRC's rankings of audit quality for a time. Since then, the firm has changed its bonus structure for partners so that audit quality is now a key measure on which their pay is determined. The FT reported that it far outweighed other metrics, such as attracting and retaining clients or relationships with colleagues. We can't confirm those findings. But that FT article also said that KPMG, which this year came bottom of the FRC rankings, also changed its bonus structure last year, removing any incentive for partners to sell non-audit services to clients, and putting more emphasis on audit quality when assessing performance. The overriding issue is that revenue growth is still king whatever the tweaking of the bonus system. If a partner cannot attract and maintain clients, he or she will not go far. The cap on non-audit work does not apply to non-listed companies or non-PIEs. There are also calls for these restrictions to be applied to non-listed companies and private companies – much loved by the private equity firms. And for once there is mention of scale fees.

Some of the problems that arise are conflicts in the accounting standards and legal rules. The difference between fair value and the legal basis of prudence is a 'true and fair view'. We explore these issues in the volume *Disruption in Financial Reporting* in this series. The focus seems to have switched from weakening prudence to providing a higher priority for the up-side. Is the true and fair view of a higher order than fair value? It should be but it seems these two concepts have become muddled. So:

1) In an effort to put pressure on the audit firms to improve audit quality, some combination of *litigation and insurance* has to be resolved eventually, however slight. We should probably rule these out – the

benefits do not outweigh the industry opposition. Otherwise we suggest combining this with some level of cap or formulaic limitation, together with insurance regulation and mandatory excesses. Combining a guarantee with the insurance option is a similar solution. These options are still a realistic possibility but very unpopular. And they are considered an overlap with increased FRC fines.

2) One of our two pillars for improving audit quality includes *a separate body in charge of deciding which auditor.* We like the idea of the FRC or equivalent running the tendering process with management present and providing input, but with the FRC making the final choice. Or provide flexibility for the boards of companies; the FRC could provide a choice of two (or three) of the Big Four (where permissible) and then let the tendering process go forward. Or, the final choice, perhaps, could be a combination of the FRC and the board (in reality the CFO and the Chairman of the Audit Committee), and taken in view of the final submissions (written). That would take the element of personal relationships and cosiness out of the equation. FRC could add the mid-tier firms to their choice for the tendering process.

3) Our second pillar is *scale fees.* These could be introduced with flexibility for reach, depth, scope, complexity and so on. This would remove the monetary relationship – someone else chooses and the fee is standardized. This proposal would need further refinement but we do not see many downsides in practice. Unfortunately, we do not think the listed companies or the FRC would favour this solution which is a pity. So it remains far-fetched and remote, but still an elegant solution. Finally as part of the FRC choosing a scale fee, we think that it would be useful to have a standardized model contract which can be tailored to cater for the special conditions of any group or company.

Additional audit and consulting choice so that we have greater independence (higher quality) and can tackle the 'insufficient numbers' issue. This is more of a shot in the dark as we have criticized this possibility of bolstering the mid-tier or challenger firms. Nevertheless it remains a possibility to provide sufficient choice. In this option, BDO and GT would need to be built up in some interventionist fashion. Also, in order to avoid a further Carillion-type situation, the consulting side of the smaller firms would need to be enhanced, perhaps through government subsidies and contracts in order to redistribute some of the consulting business away from the Big Four. Unfortunately, we cannot see this happening. The CMA sees this happening through joint audits (adding additional fees to the smaller firms). This, however, ignores the fact the the Big Four are also growing.

In Table 10.1 we can run the impact of each alternative and evaluate them in terms of our quality axioms. For example, the audit only does not change size. There is no increased competition except audit add-on work which might be undertaken by the 'audit-only' firm or the consultancy firm. The impact on independence is possibly zero – no change – though

Table 10.1 Evaluation of alternatives considering audit quality

	Axioms for higher audit quality		
	Size	*Increased competition*	*Greater Independence*
1) Big Eight and Four consulting divisions	Smaller = Negative	More firms = Positive	Neutral
2) Audit only	No change	Possibly on audit add-ons which might overlap	Mostly Neutral
3) Bolster mid-tier, share resources	Not unless they grow	More firms = Positive	Neutral
4) Share resources with the mid-tier	No change	More firms = Positive	Neutral
5) Litigation and insurance	No change	No change	Neutral
6) Someone else chooses the auditor	No change	No change	Step towards greater independence = Positive
7) Scale fees	No change	No change	Step towards greater independence = Positive
8) = 6) and 7) Someone else chooses auditor and/ or scale fees	No change	No change	Order of magnitude step towards greater independence = Positive
9) Additional audit and consulting choice	Possibly positive	More firms = Positive	Neutral
10) = 8) and 9) plus additional audit and consulting choice	Possibly positive	More firms = Positive	Order of magnitude step towards greater independence = Positive

at the margin for those add-ons there is a little additional competition but probably not enough to change audit quality. Many of the options result in smaller size or the same size audit firms. Bolstering the mid-tier and/or growing their consulting divisions might impact on size, but both would take many years. There are many options to increase competition but they all rely on splitting the Big Four in some way or bolstering the mid-tier firms until they grow to a reasonable size. Greater independence is only achieved if a) someone else chooses the auditor and/or b) scale fees are introduced.

Higher quality

The FRC noted a decline in audit quality in 2018.[4] The FRC also fined PwC their maximum of £10m for work undertaken for BHS (settled at £6.5m). In past cases, the FRC has often featured two general criticisms:

1) Failure to obtain sufficient appropriate audit evidence.
2) Failure to exercise sufficient professional scepticism.

Usually in past cases there are other factors. For example in the RSM case the FRC identified the above two criticisms and also specific issues as follows:

- the accrual of bonus payments;
- the recognition of work in progress and amounts recoverable on contracts;
- the recognition of prepaid fees for the purpose of obtaining IVA appointments;
- the classification as operating leases of two leases entered into between RSM Tenon and a business called Econocom;
- the assessment of the impairment of goodwill; and
- the preparation of the financial statements on a going-concern basis.

Our quality axioms dictate that two issues be addressed:

- **Increased competition**

   This means more firms. The fastest way to achieve this is to split the Big Four audit firms into the Big Eight but this is extremely difficult to achieve.

- **Greater independence**

   Someone else makes the choice of auditor and scale fees are introduced.

In the absence of a fundamental change there are some more short-term factors which might help. The possibilities identified previously for placing increased pressure on the Big Four include:

1) Some form of liability or insurance with excess (both suitably capped) might help though we doubt it would be very effective. In Chapter 5, we discussed a number of possible recommendations by the Kingman Review. Giving more power to the FRC (or its replacement ARGA) with greater fines, and the ability to apply the breach of a rule to:

   a) all directors of a board (including those without an accounting qualification [but that fact should be taken into account]) (not completely adopted by the Kingman Review);
   b) possibly senior staff involved in the preparation of annual and corporate reports; and any other messaging to the stock markets (e.g. trading updates or profit warning);
   c) as well as auditors (= the FRC sanction as of now).

There are two other issues which we would like to see discussed further:

1) The equivalent of an airliner crash disaster notice could be disseminated to the Big Four and other auditors. Errors, problems, mistakes, misconduct and so on could be spread by the FRC. But this would have to be much faster than now, although it could take the form of a provisional conclusion which may be confidential/anonymized.
2) FRC sanctions could include a 'name and shame' element of all personnel involved in audits that went wrong or were considered poor quality by the FRC. But Big Four personnel claim that they already feel too much pressure.

Priorities

Size

There is no general desire to change this apart from building up the mid-tier or challenger firms which might be difficult to do unless with the tacit approval of the Big Four.

Audit tenure

Axiom 2 states that higher audit quality is linked to shorter length of audit tenure. Now reducing the length of tenure (UK 20 years) is desirable for audit quality (however tenuous) but would hit the 'insufficient numbers' issue. Until that is resolved, no shortening of the audit tenure period would be possible in the UK.

More choice (more number of firms) = more competition
(and hence quality)

In practice the 'split into audit-only and consultancy' solution provides more freedom of choice. Splitting the auditing or consulting firms adds to that choice but is almost impossibly complex. Any split of the Big Four may also run into international network problems.

Current situation: the Big Four have headed off this solution so far but it may return if there is another big failure. The insufficient numbers issue remains.

The banning of non-audit work for audit clients, now adopted (in theory) by three of the Big Four is entirely different and actually limits the freedom of choice and hence increases the insufficient numbers problem. See Appendix 1.09.1 in www.fin-rep.org

Independence (and hence audit quality)

The permanent solutions to the insufficient numbers problem do not necessarily lead to a much greater degree of independence. There are two practical solutions – the second is more difficult to achieve than the first:

1) Scale fees to be set by the FRC or some watchdog in consultation with the Big Four (or their replacements). Those fees would vary according to complexity. Ex-post adjustment when some difficulties or complexities were not envisaged could be a possibility.
2) Someone else (e.g. the FRC) chooses the auditor, taking the element of personal relationships and cosiness out of the equation. The FRC could add the mid-tier firms to their choices for the tendering process.

Realistically the second alternative is probably a step too far at least initially. However, scale fees are a possibility. Also there is a body of evidence of what audit fees have been over time. Where the Big Four might argue that they have subsidized the audit work with non-audit services, that could be taken into account, as well as the second year after tendering double digit increase.

Downside: we cannot see the Big Four voluntarily agreeing so some sort of legislation would be necessary.

Current situation: the Big Four will actively resist these types of solutions. But if forced they would make a good job of this level of greater independence.

Which alternatives dominate?

No single alternative previously evaluated dominates all others. The split audit/consultancy approach provides an order of magnitude of more choice – even if postponed for now. We think that some combination of solutions would be good to address John's desire for more independence, particularly a fee scale (to be made by the FRC or its replacement) with suitable flexibility.

This is entirely different from the banning of consultancy work and undertaking audit-only work for the largest clients. As adopted by three out of the Four. Only Deloitte has not agreed and surely the firm will ultimately. Such actions actually reduces the degree of freedom of choice. See Appendix 1.09.1.

The possibility of suing auditors in some shape or form should be investigated. Obviously it requires a legal framework and would need to be limited in scope and extent. Insurance could be introduced with caps, excesses and limitations. Claims would also have to be capped to avoid claims in the billions of pounds region, which might put the survival of the firm at stake. The counterargument is that it could double up on fines by the FRC – a culpable audit firm might receive a hefty fine from the FRC and a liability claim from the courts, hence a type of double penalty.

So large fines (up from £10m to much higher levels) and the possibility of being sued may be an either/or situation. If taken together, then any fine by the FRC should be viewed or modified in the context of any settlement or court decision for damages or other monetary claim. If viewed as an alternative to being sued, the fines should be an order of magnitude larger and also issued more frequently.

We are not recommending doing damage to the Big Four, but our evidence shows that presently fines are little more than a pin prick (although the Big Four dispute this). Our evidence suggests the FRC's review and interrogation of staff changes and salary increases are far more threatening within a firm; it hits senior personnel and is taken much more seriously. Individual fines to audit staff are insignificant as all senior staff will be covered by profession indemnity insurance (like doctors). Sanctions and reprimands to senior audit staff have a significantly greater impact through peer group pressure and the impact on rewards/promotions.

The culture within all of the Big Four is to conduct their audits to the highest possible quality level. It is just that the scope, levels and tests are insufficient and no longer relevant. We discuss this in more detail in *Disruption in Auditing*.

Nearly the last word – voluntary solutions

Of the two issues which may force change sooner rather than later, 'another big failure' cannot be predicted easily or precisely. However, the 'insufficient numbers' issues will inevitably return. It may hit the US and the UK/EU at the same time. The US is not immune to these problems although the liability claims soften the consequences.

In spite of all the network, international, legal and organizational difficulties, the splitting up of the Big Four will inevitably return to the agenda in some shape or form. It would not necessarily affect the EU where joint audits are more common, and/or the US which is already diverging from UK and EU accounting/auditing standards and regulations. In time, the US and the EU might regard the 'insufficient numbers' issue as important, or the power of the Big Four may be questioned globally as it has begun to be:

> The unchecked power of the 'Big Four' accountancy firms is causing increasing unease among policymakers worldwide.[5]

So it may not be a uniquely UK-only solution. However, even if it was, the UK accounting and auditing function have always been global pioneers. We think that the Big Four would jump before they were pushed, perhaps by creating some sort of split that they would find less disrupting. In terms of time frame, our guess is that it has to be before 2030, and may be as early as the low 2020s. We envisage that such a break-up would take several years to evolve and solidify. The earliest we believe that is practical to complete such a split and be operational may be 2025.

If the Big Four were to organize a split voluntarily, we can imagine a number of scenarios. One might be to have, for example, PwC Audit A and PwC Audit B split by buildings and organizational structure with the consulting arms kept separate and perhaps, in this example, one might envisage PwC Consulting, PwC Tax and Valuation services and so on. A small administrative central section could cover all the split firms for liaison work with other country networks and also for filing purposes – though each division would also have its own published financial statements and reports. That central unit would coordinate policies and procedures. We are sure that the Big Four could come up with many more innovative possibilities providing more choice, and manage the split on their own terms.

The CMA supported the additional regulatory scrutiny of audit committees. (We oppose this as we have found that the NEDs often do not have the time or the inclination to take their NED jobs seriously). The CMA liked the concept of dual audits. (We found evidence that audit quality fell and costs increased). The CMA wanted to bolster the mid-tier challenger firms to grow in size and perhaps sharing resources with the Big Four. (We have shown that this might take decades). Finally there was a peer group remedy. The CMA was not in favour of a market share cap or breaking up-the Big Four in any way. So the insufficient numbers problem relating to the Big Four remains.

The final outcome of the CMA and ARGA is going to present a significantly tougher environment. Whatever happens from now on? We suspect that the changes to audit, company regulations, and the audit market is going to make the audit environment much tougher for the Big Four and the mid-tier challengers.

In fairness to KPMG (probably in most trouble from 2018 audit performance), they have taken some action. The reward structure for partners is now linked to audit quality. KPMG has also banned consultancy work for their largest audit clients. Both actions may take some time to be fully implemented or to be effective, but it is the cultural message that is a start. Others of the Big Four will, or have followed. Is it enough? This question is answered in the next volume: *Disruption in Financial Reporting.*

However, with the Brydon report on auditing to come and a new powerful ARGA with real teeth monitoring audits, and eventual some weak reorganizations and new controls on the Big Four arising from the CMA (perhaps), something has to change. The ICAEW is giving a series of seminars on auditing in 2019. However, the key message of all these prongs of attack on the current state of auditing is clear. These strands all support our views. All the regulators, any changes in laws and regulations are likely to take a fresh look at greater scepticism, greater independence, and the additional collection of more audit evidence. Any auditor trying to accept management estimates or accepting the top end of a range of values when only the top is supported by management - and the evidence tends to support a much lower figure - will not remain an auditor for long. This may be by 2020 or a little later. May be, just may be, this might prevent a Carillion beyond the point of no return when it was too late to save the company. Would it have saved Patisserie Valerie? (see www.fin-rep.org), Probably not. Other audit actions need to be taken. See *Disruption in Auditing.*

Could Carillion happen again? Definitely as of the date of publication, Interserve (with 68,000 employees [GT the auditors]), was a competitor with Carillion in the Government outsourcing and construction sector. In March 2019, the company went into a pre-pack sale (in effect administration and then immediate sale) to lenders - organized by EY the administrators. Surprisingly the company was brought down by the US hedge fund Coltrane Asset Management, and other shareholders rejecting management's refinancing offer. This pre-pack sale wipes out any shareholder value but the company may survive under new lender appointed management. However, the likelihood is that it will be broken up and sold in bits (as a distressed sale) with some parts of the company being closed. That said, Interserve sees their future differently.

Notes

1 White, S., Sweet, P., Smith, P., and Austin, A., 2018, 'AQIs 2018: How the major accounting firms performed in annual audit inspections', *Accountancy Daily Magazine*, 25 June 2018. Available at: www.accountancydaily.co/aqis-2018-how-major-accounting-firms-performed-annual-audit-inspections Accessed July 2018.

2 The FT articles can be found under accountancy from August to September. Accountancy articles, *Financial Times*, 2018. Available at: www.ft.com/accountancy Accessed September 2018.

3 Marriage, M., and Ford, J. 'A dangerous dance: when auditors are too close to the client: Firms can be too focused on pleasing customers who are also a source of consulting income', *Financial Times*, 28 August 2018. Available at: www.ft.com/content/29a029a0-a7b2-11e8-8ecf-a7ae1beff35b Accessed September 2018.

4 Financial Reporting Council News, 2018, 'Big Four Audit Quality Review results decline', *Financial Reporting Council*, 18 June 2018. Available at: www.frc.org.uk/news/june-2018/big-four-audit-quality-review-results-decline Accessed July 2018.

5 Carthy, M., 2018, 'Reining in the "Big Four" accountancy giants', *EU Observer*, 10 July 2018. Available at: https://euobserver.com/opinion/142319 Accessed July 2018.

Glossary

AAPA	Association of Authorised Public Accountants
AAT	The Association of Accounting Technicians
ACC	Audit Committee Chair
ACCA	Association of Chartered Certified Accountants
accountant-preparer	A qualified accountant in the firm preparing the reports, usually a financial director or CFO or a member of the board of directors
ACFE	Association of Certified Fraud Examiners
AFR	Annual financial report
AGM	An annual general meeting is a meeting of the general shareholders of a company
AI	Artificial intelligence
AIA	The Association of International Accountants
AIM	Alternative Investment Market; the Alternative Investment Market is the London Stock Exchange's global market for smaller and growing companies
AIU	Audit Inspection Unit, part of FRC
APMs	Alternative Performance Measures; a financial measure of historical or future financial performance, financial position or cash flows, other than a financial measure defined or specified in the applicable financial reporting framework
AQR	Audit Quality Review (FRC)
ARC	Audit Registration Committee (ICAEW and ICAS term)
ARC	Accounting Regulatory Committee provides opinion to the European Commission on proposals adopting IFRS and other accounting regulations

ARD	Audit Regulation Directive
ARGA	FRC's replacement. The Audit, Reporting and Governance Authority.
ASC	US Accounting Standards Codification
ASSC	Accounting Standards Steering Committee
BDO	BDO or Binder Dijker Otte is a mid-tier UK adducting firm
BEIS	Department for Business, Energy & Industrial Strategy
Big Four	PwC, Deloitte, KPMG and EY; previously also Arthur Andersen.
Black Swan event	Unexpected and unpredictable external event leading to a sudden and major upheaval, e.g. the Global Financial Crisis (see GFC)
bps	basis points
CAI	Institute of Chartered Accountants in Ireland
CBI	The Confederation of British Industry; a UK business lobbying organization
CEAOB	Committee of European Auditing Oversight Bodies
CEO	Chief Executive Officer
CESR	Committee of European Securities Regulators
CFA	Chartered Financial Analyst; CFA Institute is a global association of investment professionals
CFO	Chief Financial Officer
CIMA	Chartered Institute of Management Accountants
CIPFA	Chartered Institute of Public Finance and Accountancy
CMA	The Competition and Markets Authority; a government department in the UK, responsible for strengthening business competition and preventing and reducing anti-competitive activities. Previously the Competition Commission
CPA	Certified Public Accountant in the US
CPFA	Committee of Public Finance and Accounting
CRR	Corporate reporting review (FRC)
CSR	Corporate Social Responsibility
Deloitte	One of the Big Four accounting/auditing firms
director-preparer	Board member who is not a qualified accountant and as such is responsible for the annual reports
DPA	Deferred prosecution agreement

DTR	FCA's Disclosure and Transparency Rules
ED	Accounting Exposure Drafts
EEA	European Economic Area; includes EU countries and also Iceland, Liechtenstein and Norway. EAA countries are part of the EU's single market
EFRAG	European Financial Reporting Advisory Group
ES	Ethics Standard
ESA	European Supervisory Authority
ESG	The Environmental, Social and Governance; a set of standards for a company's operations that investors can use to screen investments
ESMA	European Securities and Markets Authority; an independent EU authority whose purpose is to improve investor protection and promote stable, orderly financial markets
EY	One of the Big Four accounting/auditing firms, formerly Ernst & Young
FANG, FAANG	Facebook, Apple, Amazon, Netflix and Alphabet/Google; acronym for the major tech firms
FAS	Statement of Financial Accounting Standards for the US
FASB	The US Financial Accounting Standards Board (FASB) is a private, non-profit organization standard-setting body whose primary purpose is to establish and improve generally accepted accounting principles (GAAP) within the United States in the public's interest
FBU	Fair, balanced and understandable
FCA	Financial Conduct Authority, a UK regulatory body; see also FRC
FED	US Federal Reserve Board – the US national bank
financial instrument	Financial instruments are assets that can be traded. They can also be seen as packages of capital that may be traded. These assets can be cash, a contractual right to deliver or receive cash or another type of financial instrument, or evidence of one's ownership of an entity
FRB	US Federal Reserve Board – the US national bank

FRC	Financial Reporting Council; one of two UK regulatory bodies, the other being the FCA
FRS	Financial Reporting Standard of the FRC applicable to the UK
FRSC	Financial Reporting Standard Council (South Africa)
FSA	UK's financial services authority, predecessor to the FCA
FSMA	The Financial Services and Markets Act 2000 – amended over the years and now incorporating (some of) MiFID – brackets our interpretation
FT	The *Financial Times*
FTSE	The Financial Times Stock Exchange share index
FTSE100	A share index of the top 100 companies listed on the London Stock Exchange with the highest market capitalization
FTSE250	The FTSE 250 Index is a capitalization-weighted index consisting of the 101st to the 350th largest companies listed on the London Stock Exchange
FTSE350	Combination of the FTSE 100 Index of the largest 100 companies and the FTSE 250 Index of the next largest 250; the largest 350 UK companies
GAAP	Generally accepted accounting principles
GAAP UK	Generally Accepted Accounting Practice in the UK
GDPR	The EU General Data Protection Regulation (GDPR); supersedes the UK Data Protection Act 1998. It brings a 21st-century approach to data protection
GFC	Global Financial Crisis (2007–2009)
GRI	Global Reporting Initiative; GRI is an independent international organization that has pioneered sustainability reporting since 1997
GT (Grant Thornton)	An unofficial abbreviation of Grant Thornton, a mid-tier UK auditing firm; fifth after the Big Four
HBOS	Halifax, Bank of Scotland
HRMC	Her Majesty's Revenue and Customs; a non-ministerial department of the UK government

responsible for the collection of taxes, the payment of some forms of state support and the administration of other regulatory regimes

HSBC
: British multinational bank with its origins in Hong Kong; originally stood for Hong Kong and Shanghai Banking Corporation

IAASB
: International Auditing and Assurance Standards Board; an independent standard-setting body that serves the public interest by setting high-quality international standards for auditing, quality control, review, other assurance and related services, and by facilitating the convergence of international and national standards

IAS
: International Accounting Standard; part of the global effort to harmonize accounting standards. Issued by IASC (the predecessor of IASB), they are still in use today and are referred to as International Accounting Standards (IAS), while standards issued by IASB are called IFRS

IASB
: International Accounting Standards Board; IASB took over the responsibility for setting International Accounting Standards from the IASC. The new board adopted existing IAS and Standing Interpretations Committee standards (SICs). The IASB has continued to develop standards, which are called "International Financial Reporting Standards" or IFRS

IASC
: International Accounting Standards Committee. Standards that were issued by IASC (the predecessor of IASB) are still within use today and go by the name International Accounting Standards (IAS),

ICAEW
: The Institute of Chartered Accountants in England and Wales, often considered as the premier professional body for accounting and audit in England and Wales

ICO
: An initial coin offering; a controversial means of crowdfunding centred around cryptocurrency, which can be a source of capital for start-up companies. In an ICO, a quantity of the crowdfunded cryptocurrency is sold to investors in

	the form of 'tokens', in exchange for legal tender or other cryptocurrencies
ICSA	The Institute of Chartered Secretaries and Administrators. ICSA: The Governance Institute is the professional body for governance
IESBA	International Ethics Standards Board for Accountants – an independent body that sets robust, internationally appropriate ethics standards, including auditor independence requirements, compiled in the Code of Ethics for Professional Accountants
IFAC	The International Federation of Accountants
IFIAR	International Forum of Independent Audit Regulators
IFRS	The International Financial Reporting Standards, usually called the IFRS Standards, are standards issued by the IFRS Foundation and the International Accounting Standards Board (IASB) to provide a common global language for business affairs
IIA	Institute of Internal Auditors
IIRC	The International Integrated Reporting Council
INEs	Independent Non-Executives
IOSCO	The International Organization of Securities Commissions
ISA (UK)	International Standards on Auditing (UK)
ISA	International Standard on Auditing; International Standards on Auditing (ISA) are professional standards for the performance of financial audit of financial information. These standards are issued by International Federation of Accountants (IFAC) through the International Auditing and Assurance Standards Board (IAASB)
ITS	Implementing Technical Standards – usually in connection with MiFID or electronic format of annual reports
KPMG	One of the Big Four accounting/auditing firms; formerly Klynveld Peat Marwick Goerdeler
Leverage	Loans and borrowed money. The greater the leverage the greater the debt as a proportion of the firm as a whole

LLA	Auditor Liability Limitation Agreements
LLP	Limited Liability Partnerships. With this form of partnership, there is limited personal liability for individual partners (similar in manner to a limited company). For tax purposes, an LLP does not differ greatly from an ordinary partnership
LSE Main Market	London Stock Exchange. International market for the admission and trading of equity, debt and other securities
M&A	Mergers and acquisitions
MAO	Modified Audit Opinion
MFR	Mandatory audit firm rotation applying to audit firms which in practice means that every seven years the audit has to go to tender
MP	Member of Parliament (UK)
MTM	Mark-to-market (MTM or M2M)
NAO	The National Audit Office; an independent Parliamentary body in the UK responsible for auditing central government departments, government agencies and non-departmental public bodies; also carries out Value for Money (VFM) audit into the administration of public policy
NAS	Non-audit services
NED	Non-executive director; also known as INE
NFI	Non-financial information
NOFA	National Organization for Financial Accounting and Reporting
non-audit services	Non-audit services comprise any engagement in which an audit firm provides professional services to: an audited entity, an audited entity's affiliates or another entity in respect of the audited entity, other than the audit of financial statements of the audited entity
P&L	Profit and Loss account also known as the income statement
P/E ratio	Price earnings ratio
PCAOB	The Public Company Accounting Oversight Board
PFI	Private Finance Initiative – see PPP for a full explanation
PIE	Public interest entity originally defined by the EU for audit purposes

plc or PLC	Public limited company (used in the UK). It is a limited liability company whose shares may be freely sold and traded to the public (although a plc may also be privately held, often by another plc), with a minimum share capital of £50,000
PPI	Public-private investment – see below
PPP	Public-private partnership is a funding model for a public infrastructure project such as a new telecommunications system, airport or power plant. The public partner is represented by the government at a local, state and/or national level
PR	Public Relations
PRA	The Prudential Regulation Authority; based in the Bank of England responsible for the regulation and supervision of 1,500 banks, building societies, credit unions, insurers and major investment firms
PRC	Planning and Resources Committee
preparer-director	Board member who is not a qualified accountant and as such is responsible for the annual reports
preparer-accountant	Preparer-account is a qualified accountant in the firm preparing the reports, usually a financial director or CFO
Principals	Partners or members of an LLP
PwC	PricewaterhouseCoopers is one of the Big Four accounting/auditing firms. Best known brandname of the Big Four
RBS	Royal Bank of Scotland – also owns NatWest Bank
Revenue	The same as turnover
rights issue	An issue of shares offered at a special price by a company to its existing shareholders in proportion to their holding of old shares. Often cashstrapped companies can turn to rights issues to raise money when they really need it. In these rights offerings, companies grant the existing shareholders a chance to buy new shares at a discount to the current trading price
RQB	Recognised Qualifying Bodies – there are six bodies in the UK recognized to offer the audit

	qualification in line with the requirements of Schedule 11 to the Companies Act 2006
RSB	Recognised Supervisory Bodies – these bodies can register and supervise audit firms in accordance with the requirements of Schedule 10 to the Companies Act 2006
RTS	Regulatory Technical Standard specifying the electronic reporting format in which issuers should prepare their annual financial reports for listed companies from 1 January 2020
S&P 500	The Standard & Poor's 500 is an American stock market index based on the market capitalizations of 500 large companies having common stock listed on the NYSE or NASDAQ. The S&P 500 index components and their weightings are determined by S&P Dow Jones indices
SASB	Sustainability Accounting Standards Board
SC	Joint report from the Business, Energy and Industrial Strategy and Work and Pensions Select Committees on Carillion
SEC	Securities and Exchange Commission. The Securities and Exchange Commission (SEC) is a US government agency that oversees securities transactions, activities of financial professionals and mutual fund trading to prevent fraud and intentional deception
SFAS	Statement of Financial Accounting Standards for the US
SFO	Serious Fraud Office
SME	A small or medium-sized enterprise; a business or company that has fewer than 250 employees; and has either (a) annual turnover not exceeding €50 million or (b) an annual balance sheet total not exceeding €43 million
SORPs	Statements of Recommended Practice
SOX	Sarbanes–Oxley Act of 2002
SPV	Special Purpose Vehicle
SRI	Socially Responsible Investors or Investment
TOR	The Onion Router for anonymous access to the dark web
TPR	The Pensions Regulator

UK GAAP	Generally accepted accounting principles and practices for the UK
UK regulated market	An organised trading venue that operates under Title III of MiFID
US GAAP	Generally accepted accounting principles for the US
VAT	Value Added Tax; a common sales tax throughout the EU

Printed in the United States
by Baker & Taylor Publisher Services